# Cambridge Elements ≡

Elements in the Philosophy of Ludwig Wittgenstein
edited by
David G. Stern
*University of Iowa*

# WITTGENSTEIN
# ON CRITERIA AND PRACTICES

## Lars Hertzberg
*Åbo Akademi University*

CAMBRIDGE
UNIVERSITY PRESS

# CAMBRIDGE
## UNIVERSITY PRESS

Shaftesbury Road, Cambridge CB2 8EA, United Kingdom

One Liberty Plaza, 20th Floor, New York, NY 10006, USA

477 Williamstown Road, Port Melbourne, VIC 3207, Australia

314–321, 3rd Floor, Plot 3, Splendor Forum, Jasola District Centre, New Delhi – 110025, India

103 Penang Road, #05–06/07, Visioncrest Commercial, Singapore 238467

Cambridge University Press is part of Cambridge University Press & Assessment, a department of the University of Cambridge.

We share the University's mission to contribute to society through the pursuit of education, learning and research at the highest international levels of excellence.

www.cambridge.org
Information on this title: www.cambridge.org/9781108931168
DOI: 10.1017/9781108946537

First published 2022

A catalogue record for this publication is available from the British Library.

ISBN 978-1-108-93116-8 Paperback
ISSN 2632-7112 (online)
ISSN 2632-7104 (print)

# Wittgenstein on Criteria and Practices

Elements in the Philosophy of Ludwig Wittgenstein

DOI: 10.1017/9781108946537
First published online: December 2022

Lars Hertzberg
*Åbo Akademi University*
**Author for correspondence:** Lars Hertzberg, lhertzbe@abo.fi

**Abstract:** In interpretive literature from the 1950s through the 1970s, the term 'criterion' was thought to be a central key to the understanding of Wittgenstein's later philosophy. Later on, it was relegated from this place of honour to being one of a variety of expressions used by Wittgenstein in dealing with philosophical questions. This Element tries to account for the shifting fate of this concept. It discusses the various occurrences of the word 'criteria' in *Philosophical Investigations*, argues that the post-Wittgensteinian debate about criteria was put on the wrong track by a problematic passage in Wittgenstein's early *Blue Book*, and finally gives an overview of the main contributions to this debate, trying to achieve a reconciliation between the rival conceptions.

**Keywords:** Wittgenstein, criteria, practice, philosophy of mind, philosophy of language

ISBNs: 9781108931168 (PB), 9781108946537 (OC)
ISSNs: 2632-7112 (online), 2632-7104 (print)

# Contents

# Introduction

For about thirty years following the publication of Wittgenstein's *Philosophical Investigations* the concept of a criterion came to hold a central place in the discussion of his work, beginning with Norman Malcolm's review of the book in 1954.[1] To many commentators, it held the key to what was revolutionary in Wittgenstein's contribution to philosophy. However, since the early 1980s, criteria seem to have slipped rather quickly out of focus. In Wittgenstein commentaries that have appeared during the past thirty to forty years, with few exceptions, criteria are not paid much attention.[2] This shift has also taken place in the minds of individual commentators. While Malcolm was apparently the commentator who first lifted the concept to prominence, it is mentioned only in passing in his late work, *Nothing is Hidden: Wittgenstein's Criticism of his Early Thought* (1986).[3] Again, consider the work of Gordon Baker. In his essay 'Criteria: A New Foundation for Semantics', published in 1974,[4] he hailed Wittgenstein's introduction of the concept of criterion as the beginning of a revolution in the philosophy of language: an approach he termed Constructive Semantics was to replace Classical Semantics – the outlook which he claimed, no doubt with some justification, to underlie most contemporary theories of meaning (whether explicitly or not). However, in the posthumous collection of Baker's essays, mainly written in the 1990's, called *Wittgenstein's Method: Neglected Aspects,*[5] hardly any attention is given to criteria.

In this Element, I shall try to present a reading of some of the central uses of the term 'criterion' in Wittgenstein's work, focusing primarily on *Philosophical Investigations*. After that, I shall present and comment on the main issues and lines of argument in the post-Wittgensteinian debate concerning criteria. I shall conclude by proposing an account of why interest in criteria gradually faded.

What are criteria? Without forejudging the discussion to follow, let me propose a preliminary definition of the word 'criterion'. The criterion for something being so, we may say, is that which is crucial for the thing being so, this being bound up with the meaning of the claim that it is so. Thus, the criterion of a goal in football is the ball passing the goal line while in play; that is what the referee has to go by in awarding a goal to the attacking team.

---

[1] *The Philosophical Review*, 63 (1954), 530–59. Reprinted, in slightly different form, in Malcolm's collection *Knowledge and Certainty*, and in Pitcher (ed.), *Wittgenstein*: The Philosophical Investigations, 65–103. References are to the Pitcher volume.

[2] Among the few exceptions are Wright, *Realism, Meaning and Truth*, 2nd ed.; Glock, 'Criteria', 92–7; McDowell, 'Criteria, Defeasibility and Knowledge', 369–94; Hanfling, 'Criteria, Conventions and the Problem of Other Minds', 38–50; and Loomis, 'Criteria', in 160–8.

[3] Oxford: Basil Blackwell, 1986.     [4] *Ratio* 16 (1974), 156–89.

[5] Oxford: Basil Blackwell, 2004.

This is the meaning of the word 'goal' in the context of football (or, in the terminology occasionally adopted by Wittgenstein, this is part of the 'grammar' of the word 'goal' as used within the practice of playing football). If I'm outside the stadium I can tell that the home team has scored a goal by the sudden roar rising from the audience, but that is not what is *meant* by a goal in football. For another example, the criterion of a person having died is (or used to be) her heart having stopped beating. We may, of course, judge her to have died when she ceases to move or to be responsive to external stimuli, but this judgment may turn out to be mistaken, whereas the heart-beat mark may not. Here, by the way, we also have a case of criterial change: in some countries, the legal criterion of death is no longer the heart but the brain ceasing to function.

The word 'criterion' (plural 'criteria') – in German '*Kriterium*' ('*Kriterien*') – occurs very frequently in Wittgenstein's notebooks and lectures from 1929 onwards. In most of these cases, the word is used in connection with his making a point about the use of some expression, in ways seeming to take it for granted that the word will be understood without explanation. In other words, Wittgenstein is evidently reckoning with the reader's familiarity with the word.

Wittgenstein's remarks containing the word 'criterion' are not, on the whole, meant to throw light on what is meant by 'criteria'; rather, for him, talk of criteria is a tool for drawing attention to some uses of words. Wittgenstein thought it meaningful to distinguish, in clarifying the use of certain words within a practice, between the sorts of grounds for applying the word that are constitutive of the role of the word in that practice – the criteria – and the sorts of grounds that are dependent on empirical connections.

Suppose, in the course of conversation, I ask a question beginning, say, 'When do we say ... ?', or 'How does one tell ... ?', or 'What is meant by calling something ... ?' I may do so to get clear about the use of some word in the course of being introduced into a practice (or maybe to get a sharper sense of the use of some word of which I only have a vague grasp). Or, when involved in a discussion, I may ask 'When would *you* say ... ?' (etc.), perhaps because I have a notion that you and I may not be talking about the same thing. I would suggest that, when Wittgenstein talks about criteria, what he has in mind are, roughly, the answers people would give to questions like these. We might call them 'criterial claims'. (Another type of criterial claim which he also seems to have in mind at times is that of announcing a stipulation about how some word *is to be used* in the context of a practice.) I am not implying that in making criterial claims, people will typically use the word 'criterion' – nor, on the other hand, are they necessarily making this sort of claim whenever they use that word.

(As will be made clear later, in Section 5.2, criterial claims are not only used in connection with describing practices.)

Questions beginning 'How does one know . . . ?' (except where they can be replaced by questions of the first type) or 'What makes you think . . . ?' are typically not requests for criteria in this sense but rather for (empirical) evidence (or, as Wittgenstein occasionally says, 'symptoms') of something being the case – the way the roaring of the audience is evidence of the home team having scored a goal, or the way a person's being totally unresponsive and motionless may be evidence of her death.

Rogers Albritton, in an early paper on criteria, says that criteria for Wittgenstein 'are primarily criteria that men "accept", "adopt", "fix", "introduce", and "use" or "apply" in connection with their use of certain *expressions*'.[6] The emphasis here is on what Albritton calls the conventional character of criterial claims. This gives a strong emphasis to cases in which the appeal to criteria is conscious and deliberate, sometimes even a matter of choice. However, it is important to note that in many cases something being criterial is simply a given for those who participate in a practice, and that, often enough, reflection may be required for us to become aware of where we place the criterial conditions for the use of some word within a practice.

Only on a very few occasions is the word 'criterion' foregrounded in Wittgenstein's writings. This is true in particular of a passage in *The Blue Book*,[7] which came to receive a great deal of attention and seems to have guided the understanding of the word in much of the ensuing debate, in ways that are not really warranted by Wittgenstein's own actual use of the word. I shall get back to some of these 'foregrounding' remarks later, but wish to focus for now on the cases in which the word is doing yeoman work.

The word 'criterion' occurs only once in Wittgenstein's early work, the *Tractatus Logico-Philosophicus* (published in 1921)[8]:

> 6.1271 It is clear that the number of the 'primitive propositions of logic' is arbitrary, since one could derive logic from a single primitive proposition, e.g. by simply constructing the logical product of Frege's primitive propositions. (Frege would perhaps say that we should then no longer have an immediately self-evident proposition. But it is remarkable that a thinker as rigorous as Frege appealed to the degree of self-evidence as the criterion of a logical proposition.)

---

[6] 'On Wittgenstein's Use of the Term "Criterion"'. First published in *The Journal of Philosophy* 56 (1959), 845–57. Reprinted in Pitcher (ed.), *Wittgenstein:* The Philosophical Investigations, 231–50. The quotation is from p. 237.

[7] In Wittgenstein, *The Blue and Brown Books*, 1–74.

[8] Translated by Pears & McGuinness (1961).

Let me make a brief remark on this passage. 'Criterion' is here used in characterizing a position that Wittgenstein rejected. He thought, at the time, that logical truth could only be established through mechanical calculation, say, by means of truth-value tables. The idea that logical truth could be established on the basis of whether a proposition is self-evident to us would constitute a return to the psychologism that Gottlob Frege had successfully criticized, and the criticism of which had been an important influence on Wittgenstein's own thinking. Wittgenstein could conceivably have countered Frege's notion by saying that the criterion of logical truth is rather whether a proposition gets the value 'true' for all possible truth-value combinations. (For example, a proposition of the form 'p v ~p', in this strand of thought, is true whether or not the constituent proposition for which 'p' stands is true or false: 'It's either raining or not raining', it will be said, is true in all possible situations, true whether it is raining or not.)

It is not hard to see why Wittgenstein had little use for the term 'criterion' in the *Tractatus*: in that work he was interested in the formal conditions for chains of words constituting propositions and in the formal connections between propositions; on the conception he held at that time, the way we tell whether something is so had no bearing on those issues. Relations between propositions were either truth-conditional or contingent. Considerations of language use were not then part of his concern.

The one time he does use the word in the quoted passage, he is not speaking of the sense of propositions, but rather what it is to *speak about speaking* about propositions; in this case, what it means to call a proposition logically true. The remark belongs to a debate about how to construct the scaffolding for an account of language, not to the account of language itself.

I shall, then, concentrate on occurrences of the term 'criterion' in Wittgenstein's later work, in particular *Philosophical Investigations*.[9] By limiting the scope of inquiry, I hope to be able to focus on some of the central concerns in connection with which Wittgenstein used the term.

Let me briefly indicate what kind of work *Philosophical Investigations* is. As in the *Tractatus*, Wittgenstein is concerned with getting clear about issues concerning language and meaning. However, the spirit in which he approaches these issues is altogether different from that of the *Tractatus*; we might even say the issues themselves are different. Meaning is now regarded in the context of

---

[9] References to this work (previously known as 'Part I') will be given as *PI* followed by the numeral I, '§' and section number. References to *Philosophy of Psychology: A Fragment* (previously known as 'Part II'), contained in the same volume, will be given in two ways: first with the initials *'PPF'* followed by '§' and paragraph number, then by *PI* followed by the numeral II, chapter, and page number.

the different roles linguistic expressions have in the lives of the speakers of language. What is brought to the fore here is the great variety of uses of language. Whereas the concept of representation was the pivot around which the inquiry turned in the *Tractatus*, in *Philosophical Investigations* Wittgenstein does not presuppose that there is a unified notion of representation which lies at the basis of communication by means of language.

In the preface to *Philosophical Investigations*, Wittgenstein says that the thoughts in it 'concern many subjects: the concepts of meaning, of understanding, of a proposition and sentence, of logic, the foundations of mathematics, states of consciousness, and other things' (4).

He goes on to characterize his mode of proceeding as follows:

> After several unsuccessful attempts to weld my results together into ... a whole, I realized that I should never succeed. The best that I could write would never be more than philosophical remarks; my thoughts soon grew feeble if I tried to force them along a single track against their natural inclination. – And this was, of course, connected with the very nature of the investigation. For it compels us to travel criss-cross in every direction over a wide field of thought. – The philosophical remarks in this book are, as it were, a number of sketches of landscapes which were made in the course of these long and meandering journeys. (4)

According to the conception held by Wittgenstein in *Philosophical Investigations*, philosophical problems often arise because we regard the uses of words through preconceived notions, typically by disregarding the difference between uses that appear to be analogous. The temptation to do so is to be overcome by looking closely at the various uses 'despite an urge to misunderstand them' (*PI* I, §§ 66, 109). Thus, one and the same word may occur in quite different roles in different conversational contexts (e.g. 'know', 'understand', 'think', etc.). Or two words may on the surface seem to behave similarly, but their actual use may be radically different (e.g. 'say' and 'mean', § 664).

The aim of his work, it could be said, is to teach the reader how to come to terms with the seemingly intractable problems to which the words discussed give rise, by reminding ourselves of the ways they are used in common conversation. Appeals to criterial considerations belong to this job of description.

*Philosophical Investigations* was the final outcome of an extended effort to formulate a conception of philosophy which had started in the early 1930s, that is, at the time Wittgenstein returned to philosophy after an absence of almost a decade (at the same time as he returned from Vienna to Cambridge, where he had been studying before the outbreak of the war in 1914). The extensive work which has been preserved in his notebooks and typescripts from that time and until his death in 1951, was in large part work preparatory for a book he intended to publish, the nearest approximation to which is *Philosophical Investigations* as we have it today, a work that can be called final only in the sense that Wittgenstein was no longer in position to go on working on it. The book, whose German title is *Philosophische Untersuchungen*, appeared posthumously in 1953 under the editorship of the three persons Wittgenstein had designated his literary executors: Elizabeth Anscombe, Rush Rhees, and G. H. von Wright, in a bilingual edition with an English translation by Anscombe.

Wittgenstein's huge literary *Nachlass*, his notebooks, earlier compilations of his remarks, as well as notes based on his lectures have gradually been made available over the years.

*Philosophical Investigations* contains 1,065 numbered remarks (693 in Part I and 372 in *Philosophy of Psychology – A Fragment*/Part II) as well as 13 unnumbered remarks (all in Part I). The word 'criterion' ('criteria') occurs in 41 remarks, spread fairly evenly throughout the text. In 39 of those remarks, the criteria spoken about concern matters attributed to persons (sensation,[10] experience,[11] state of mind or brain,[12] understanding,[13] activity such as reading[14] or calculating in one's head,[15] mastery or ability,[16] acting correctly or making a mistake,[17] recognizing a feeling,[18] seeing,[19] a thought being complete at an earlier moment,[20] looking without seeing,[21] having an image of red[22]). The remainder concern identity of persons,[23] how a rule is meant,[24] fit (a cylinder fitting into a hollow cylinder), change of fit, change of weight,[25] rain.[26]

In twenty-one of the remarks, the word 'criterion' occurs in a question: 'what is the criterion for . . . ?' Here, Wittgenstein is evidently inviting us to reflect on what it would mean to accept something as a criterion for the word in question, or to decide what the criterion is to be. Sometimes, he is suggesting that there is no criterion; sometimes that the criteria vary between contexts. Often, settling on a criterion is a way of determining whether or not two speakers mean the same by some word in a given context.

In many cases, Wittgenstein is not telling us what *he* considers the criteria to be, rather the only authority within sight is *the reader.* The invocation of criteria is often an aid in describing this or that actual or imagined linguistic practice.

---

[10] I §§ 258, 288, 290.     [11] I §§ 239, 322, 509, 542, *PPF* § 146/IIxi, 198.
[12] I §§ 141, 149, 572, 573, *PPF* § 36/IIvi, 181.     [13] I §§ 182, 185, 269, 288.
[14] I §§ 159, 160, 164.     [15] I § 385.
[16] I §§ 159, 160, 164, 182, 185, 190, 238, 269, 385, *PPF* §§ 36, 180/IIvi, 181, xi, 203.
[17] I §§ 51, 56, 258.     [18] I § 625.     [19] *PPF* § 236/IIxi, 212.     [20] I § 633.
[21] *PPF* § 242/IIxi, 211.     [22] I § 377.     [23] I § 404.     [24] I §§ 190, 692.     [25] All I § 182.
[26] I § 354.

A request for criteria may be a way of challenging the reader to account for the way she conceives of a real or imaginary practice, how words are used or how they might be used. Unless we are able to specify the criteria for the use of a word, we may have failed to describe a practice. I think the emphasis on practice is important here. Rather than being connected with certain words or sentences considered in the abstract, I would suggest, criteria are connected with the way words or sentences are used within a given practice; within a different practice, the same word or sentence may be bound up with other criteria. (As we shall see later in Section 5.2, criteria may sometimes be thought of as tied to an individual conversational situation rather than to a practice.)

In the next section, I will choose a sample of the remarks and attempt a close reading of them, hoping to bring out some of the uses to which Wittgenstein is putting the word 'criterion'.

# 1 'Criteria' in *Philosophical Investigations*

## 1.1 Mental States

A number of times when criteria are invoked in *Philosophical Investigations*, the issue concerns the kinds of states we attribute to people, such as knowing, understanding, remembering, expecting, having an opinion, and so on. Wittgenstein's purpose is to encourage us to look closely at the practices of attributing such states to people, as a way of overcoming an inclination to misconstrue them. The general theme of these remarks is well brought out in *PI* I, § 573:

> To have an opinion is a state. – A state of what? Of the soul? Of the mind? Well, what does one say has an opinion? Mr. N. N. for example. And that is the correct answer.
>
> One should not expect to be enlightened by the answer to *that* question. Other questions that go deeper are: What, in particular cases, do we regard as criteria for someone's being of such-and-such an opinion? When do we say that he reached this opinion at that time? When that he has altered his opinion? And so on. The picture that the answers to these questions give us shows *what* gets treated grammatically as a *state* here.

Wittgenstein is criticizing our inclination to think that having an opinion consists in a state of a person's *mind, soul,* or perhaps his *brain,* which can be identified independently of the ways in which the opinion is manifested in what he says and does. However, when it comes to finding out, in an actual case, whether someone has a certain opinion, when he reached it, when he altered it, and so on, it should be obvious that we would not bother about some inner (and probably unknowable) condition of the person (which may be hard or impossible to identify), but would go by things he tells us and things he does. Even if a neurologist were to argue that she could identify a state of the brain corresponding to such and such an opinion, that decision would depend on her having established a correlation between the brain state and the way the opinion is manifested in the person's words and actions. Otherwise, the claim that the brain state constituted having the opinion would be groundless. At bottom, a person's opinions are a matter of the way he lives and acts, rather than inner, inaccessible states. That seems to be Wittgenstein's point in saying that Mr N. N.'s having an opinion is a state *of Mr N. N.* rather than of his mind or brain.

Why does Wittgenstein say that this claim, though correct, may not be enlightening? Maybe because the reader is apt to think that the observation is trivial: of course, we normally attribute opinions to the people who hold them, not to their brains or minds. A person may, of course, feign opinions he does not have, but in that case we expect his true opinions to manifest themselves in other things he might do, in secret perhaps. Such suspicions, in any case, do not normally enter into our talk about people's opinions. Nevertheless, the reader may think, to speak about having an opinion as an internal (mental or neuro-logical) state may be a more 'exact' way of speaking – one that corresponds more closely to the scientific facts of the matter. In order to counteract this inclination, Wittgenstein exhorts us to look at the criteria by which we try to find out about a person's opinions: the criteria consist in things about *him*, rather than things *inside* him.

An analogous point is made in *PI* I § 149:

> If one says that knowing the ABC is a state of the mind, one is thinking of a state of an apparatus of the mind (perhaps a state of the brain) by means of which we explain the *manifestations* of that knowledge. Such a state is called a disposition. But it is not unobjectionable to speak of a state of the mind here, inasmuch as there would then have to be two different criteria for this: finding out the structure of the apparatus, as distinct from its effects. (Nothing would be more confusing here than to use the words 'conscious' and 'unconscious' for the contrast between a state of consciousness and a disposition. For this pair of terms covers up a grammatical difference.)

By 'the structure of the apparatus', Wittgenstein evidently means the condition of the mind or brain which the state of knowing the alphabet presumably consists in, whereas 'the effects' correspond to the ways that knowledge is shown. Knowing the alphabet, like the majority of states dis-cussed by Wittgenstein, involves the mastery of certain skills or the grasp of some task. Again, there is an inclination to think that, if someone knows the alphabet, that knowledge consists in a state of her mind (or brain) which *explains* her ability to do various things like recite the alphabet, find a dictionary entry by using the alphabet, write a list of names in alphabetical order, insert a book in the shelf in the correct place based on the author's name, and so on. There seem to be several reasons for assuming that such a state exists independently of actual instances of manifesting the knowledge. For one thing, the skill follows predictable patterns. A person acquires them through a certain kind of teaching, mainly through rote training, and not in some radically different way; and once they are safely acquired, they are rarely lost, except possibly after a long period of disuse or in consequence of mental deterioration. Besides, the different manifestations of the knowledge tend to go together. If someone is able to find words in a dictionary we expect her to be able to list names alphabetically, and so on. Hence, someone's manifesting an alphabetical skill on one occasion provides a basis for predicting how she will perform on other occasions. Of particular importance is the fact that someone who has shown mastery of the alphabet will also be trusted with the competence to judge whether another person is able to recite the alphabet correctly and whether she is able to employ her knowledge of the alphabet consistently and to good purpose, and so on.

These facts – that alphabetic competence tends to retain a degree of consistency, and that various forms of it tend to be combined in one and the same person – are known from our experience of the ways in which 'knowledge of the alphabet' normally manifests itself in human life. Apart from this, like all attributions of mastery, attribution of this knowledge has the *grammatical* form of an assertion about a state, just as attributions of opinions have the form of assertions about the state of a person. People are said to possess the knowledge, not only while actually making use of it, but over time, on the basis of having used it successfully on earlier occasions – provided they have not lost it. It is natural, then, to think that if the attribution of knowledge is to have meaning, there must be something for the knowledge to *consist in* even when a person is not employing it – something over and above those employments – or else, it seems, a person's retaining the relevant skills would be a mystery. Indeed, it might even be thought that to treat human abilities as consisting in states residing in the mind or brain is the strictly scientific way of talking about them, whereas referring to them as constituted by the disposition to succeed in performing certain tasks is a way of talking that, while it may get us by in our everyday concerns, is imprecise and does not fulfil any more ambitious purposes.[27]

---

[27] For instance, it would not enable us to say exactly at what point in time a person has learnt to read.

Let us suppose, however, that such an independent (say, brain) state does exist. What would it mean to call it the state of knowing the alphabet? The connection between this state and its manifestations would evidently be causal. But a causal connection would depend on other circumstances being normal. Suppose that, under certain conditions, being in that brain state did not ensure the ability to employ the alphabet (e.g. the state would remain the same even after one lost the ability) would we still call it 'knowledge of the alphabet'? Well, if someone were to start using the expression 'knowing the alphabet' in that way, he would no longer be using it the way people usually do. Normally we would say that a person's knowledge of the alphabet is tested by asking her to perform the kinds of chores listed here. But someone who started talking in the new way might be saying things like, 'I don't know if she knows the alphabet, all I know is she can recite and list names in alphabetical order,' or 'He does have knowledge of the alphabet, he simply lacks the ability to employ it.' What are we to say here? In the way we normally speak about knowledge of the alphabet, this knowledge has no independent identity apart from its tending to manifest itself in characteristic ways.[28]

Someone might ask why we should not reform our ways of talking and decide to let the vocabulary by which we talk about different forms of mastery take the form of the naming of inner states, and change the criteria accordingly. Now, an objection to this proposal is that, apart from the obvious fact that our knowledge of the mind or brain is far too limited for us even to imagine identifying specific conditions as being (more or less consistently) correlated with various forms of knowing or understanding, and so on, such a proposal is totally oblivious to the role of various assessments of knowledge, remembering, understanding, and so on, in our life. When I wonder whether someone knows the alphabet, my interest may be, for instance, in whether I can entrust her with certain tasks, not what state her brain is in (cf. *PI* I, § 158). This is reflected in the criteria we employ. It may be held, perhaps, that the foremost purpose of speaking is simply to record how things are in the world, and thus an account of human abilities in terms of neurological conditions might be taken to provide a more exact representation of reality than one relying on successful performances. However, this argument ignores the fact that there is a variety of ways in which the state of things may be recorded and there is no ground for elevating any one of them above the others. Hence, there is no objective reason for calling a characterization of a human being, say, in terms of brain states more important or correct than a characterization in terms of her ways of acting.

---

[28] To point this out is not, of course, to deny that a functioning brain is a precondition for performing the kinds of things that show one knows the alphabet; the point is simply that this knowledge cannot be identified with some specific state of the brain.

In brief, it may be said that knowledge of the alphabet, as it is normally spoken of, does not presuppose the existence of some independently identifiable state. There is nothing that has to endure continually throughout the time during which someone knows the alphabet – apart, we might say, from *her knowing the alphabet*. Consider the way we talk about the duration of a state. If I suffer from tinnitus, I may be asked whether I hear the sound the whole time, or only intermittently. I might reply that the sound ceased at a certain point in time and started again at such and such a time. I could answer the question whether the sound is there when I'm sleeping or only when I'm awake. But with things like knowing the alphabet, we do not ask such questions. And the same for knowing how to play chess, understanding how to continue a number series, being able to speak French, and so on. We do not talk about the duration of abilities in the same way as we talk about the duration of a bodily state or a sensation. This question is discussed in *PI* I, § 182:

> The grammar of 'to fit', 'to be able', and 'to understand'. Exercises: (1) When is a cylinder C said to fit into a hollow cylinder H? Only as long as C is inside H? (2) Sometimes one says: C has ceased to fit into H at such and such a time. What criteria are used in such a case for its having happened at that time? (3) What does one regard as criteria for a body's having changed its weight at a particular time, if it was not actually on the balance at that time? (4) Yesterday I knew the poem by heart; today I no longer know it. In what kind of case does it make sense to ask: 'When did I stop knowing it by heart?' (5) Someone asks me 'Can you lift this weight?' I answer 'Yes'. Now he says 'Do it!' – and I can't. In what kind of circumstances would one accept the excuse 'When I answered "yes" I *could* do it, only now I can't'?
>
> The criteria which we accept for 'fitting', 'being able to', 'understanding', are much more complicated than might appear at first sight. That is, the game with these words, their use in the linguistic intercourse that is carried on by their means, is more involved – the role of these words in our language is other than we are tempted to think.
>
> (This role is what we need to understand in order to resolve philosophical paradoxes. And that's why definitions usually aren't enough to resolve them; and even less so the statement that a word is 'indefinable'.)

If I read Wittgenstein correctly here, he is giving instances of cases in which timing a change of state would be problematic. This is true both in the case of some physical states and in the case of some physical and mental abilities. For one thing, it might be said, the timing of these changes of state will rarely be an issue, and if it ever does become an issue, resolving it would mostly not be straightforward. Here we may have no criteria ready to hand. Perhaps a change in a state of fit or the weight of a product could be a matter of contention between a seller and a buyer. The buyer might complain, say, that a leg of mutton weighed less than what was said on the label, and the seller might have to account for the discrepancy in terms of some unforeseen change that had taken place between the labelling of the produce and its delivery, in order to uphold his claim to have been acting in good faith. In this case, the explanation would depend on our knowledge of how such things generally happen. If this situation happened often, criteria might gradually develop.

An alternative example would be if the teacher asked which of the students had learnt the poem by heart but one of the students who raised his hand was unable to recite it. Was he just pretending to know, hoping he wouldn't be tested, or did his nerves give out, say, when he was asked to recite the poem? The matter might be hard to decide in an actual case. But then issues like these rarely arise. Suppose I recall being able to recite 'The Charge of the Light Brigade' when I went to school, but am no longer able to do so. At what point in time did I forget it? In a normal case, we would not have any idea of how to go about answering the question – indeed, we would find it hard to take the question seriously. The time of forgetting something is not the sort of thing for which criteria are normally available.

Wittgenstein's point, then, seems to be that states such as abilities are not unique in having an indeterminate duration. In the cases we have mentioned, our understanding of the question of when the change of state took place would depend on the context.

In *PI* I, § 572 Wittgenstein writes: 'Expectation is, grammatically, a state; like: being of an opinion, hoping for something, knowing something, being able to do something. But in order to understand the grammar of these states, it is necessary to ask: "What counts as a criterion for anyone's being in such a state?" (States of hardness, of weight, of fitting.)'

The words in parentheses seem to refer back to the remark we have just been discussing.

Could we imagine a language in which, say, knowing the alphabet would not be talked about grammatically as a state? In a given situation, we would say that someone was reciting the alphabet, that she was putting a list of names in alphabetical order, and so on, but we would not say that she knew the alphabet. Rather than 'teaching' someone the alphabet we would talk of training a person so that she could carry out certain tasks. And so, instead of saying she knew the alphabet we would say she had been taught the alphabet. (Similarly, rather than saying that someone knew something we might say she had found it out, etc.). In having been taught the alphabet, a person could be said to have achieved a certain status, which she retained until, for some reason, she lost the ability to carry out the associated tasks. Here, the notion of a state would still play a role, although it was not made explicit. (Try to imagine, more radically still, a language in which the idea of such a status does not exist. Maybe we think that there would simply be talk about carrying out tasks, the successful performance of which would depend on the correct employment of the alphabet. However, in the absence of a notion like knowing the alphabet or the status of having been taught the alphabet, no one could claim the competence to judge whether such a task had been performed correctly, and hence the very idea of an alphabet – of a correct ordering of letters – would have no place in that language.)

## 1.2 Feeling Able

Where the exercise of skills is concerned, there is also another temptation at play, as brought out, for instance, in the following remark in *PPF* § 36/*PI* II vi, 181:

> What would we reply to someone who told us that with *him* understanding was an inner process? – What would we reply to him if he said that with him knowing how to play chess was an inner process? – We'd say that when we want to know if he can play chess, we aren't interested in anything that goes on inside him. – And if he retorts that this is in fact just what we are interested in, that is, in whether he can play chess – then we should have to draw his attention to the criteria which would demonstrate his ability, and on the other hand to the criteria for 'inner states'.
>
> Even if someone had a particular ability only when, and only as long as, he had a particular feeling, the feeling would not be the ability.

Earlier, in Part I of *Philosophical Investigations*, §§ 156–71, there is a long sequence of remarks in which Wittgenstein considers what it means to have learnt to read – at what point will we say that a pupil is able to read? This discussion can serve as a model for a number of skills. Wittgenstein writes, after considering the suggestion that being able to read is a matter of certain connections having been established in the brain:

> But when we think the matter over, we're tempted to say: the one real criterion for anybody's *reading* is the conscious act of reading, the act of reading the sounds off from the letters. 'A man surely knows whether he is reading or only pretending to read!' – Suppose A wants to make B believe that he can read Cyrillic script. He learns a Russian sentence by heart and utters it while looking at the printed words as if he were reading them. Here we'll surely say that A knows he is not reading, and has a sense of just this while pretending to read. For there are, of course, many feelings more or less characteristic of reading a printed sentence; it is not difficult to recall such feelings: think of feelings of hesitating, of looking closer, of misreading, of words following on one another in a more or less familiar fashion, and so on. And equally there are feelings characteristic of reciting something one has learnt by heart. In our example, A will have none of the feelings that are

> characteristic of reading, and will perhaps have various feelings characteristic of cheating. (*PI* I, § 159)

In other words, on reflection, someone may give up the idea that to speak about someone being able to read is to speak about something in the brain, and argue instead that it must a be matter of the feelings which accompany the act of reading. What makes it natural to assume that reading must consist in or be accompanied by a specific feeling is evidently the fact that, when reading, we are aware of doing it – of exercising this particular skill. The assumption that reading is constituted by a feeling accompanying the activity, it seems, would account for our access to what we are doing when reading: the feeling keeps us informed that we are reading. Setting ourselves to read is not just a process that suddenly takes place in us. We begin reading because we have the intention to read. The feeling that we are reading is a feeling that we master the activity we are engaged in – there is an assurance that we will be able to go on reading – just as when we know how to play chess there is an assurance that we are going to be able to move the pieces in accordance with the rules of the game. Hence the attraction of the idea that the criterion of reading or of being able to play chess is a feeling accompanying the activity.

But again, we could imagine someone being able to perform correctly while having the feeling (induced by a drug, say) that she is not reading (§ 160) – or the other way round: any specific feeling we could propose might be present – and the ability to read be absent. (I am here cutting a short line through Wittgenstein's rich and nuanced discussion of various relations between feeling and mastery.)

> 'It's as if we could grasp the whole use of a word at a stroke' – Well, that is just what we say we do. That is: we sometimes describe what we do in these words. But there is nothing astonishing, nothing strange about what happens. It becomes strange when we are led to think that the future development must in some way already be present in the act of grasping the use and yet isn't present. – For we say that there isn't any doubt that we understand the word, and on the other hand its meaning lies in its use. There is no doubt that I now want to play chess, but chess is the game it is in virtue of all its rules (and so on). Don't I know, then, which game I want to play until I have played it? Or is it rather that all the rules are contained in my act of intending? Is it experience that tells me that this sort of game usually follows such an act of intending? So can't I actually be sure what I intended to do? And if that is nonsense – what kind of super-rigid connection obtains between the act of intending and the thing intended? – Where is the connection effected between the sense of the words 'Let's play a game of chess' and all the rules of the game? – Well, in the list of rules of the game, in the teaching of it, in the everyday practice of playing. (*PI* I, § 197)

The temptation to construe the criterion of an ability along the lines of a feeling accompanying our performance plays an important part in connection with *understanding*, a topic that is extensively discussed in *Philosophical Investigations*. In I §§ 151–5, Wittgenstein discusses the case of someone being asked to try to continue a number series. A writes down the numbers 1, 5, 11, 19, 29. B tries to find a rule for the series. B may suddenly exclaim, 'Now I can go on!' Before this, while A was writing, B may have been trying out various formulae on the numbers A was writing, or asked himself, 'What is the series of differences?'; or perhaps saw directly how he was to continue, maybe with the feeling 'That's easy!'

Wittgenstein rejects the idea that any of these experiences might *be* the understanding, as any of them might be present without B having understood. Say, the formula might have hovered before B's mind without his realizing that it was indeed the right solution. Wittgenstein sums up the conundrum as follows:

> Now we try to get hold of the mental process of understanding which seems to be hidden behind those coarser and therefore more readily visible concomitant phenomena. But it doesn't work; or, more correctly, it does not get as far as a real attempt. For even supposing I had found something that happened in all those cases of understanding, why should that be the understanding? Indeed, how can the process of understanding have been hidden, given that I said 'Now I understand' because I did understand? And if I say it is hidden – then how do I know what I have to look for? I am in a muddle.
>
> – Just for once, don't think of understanding as a 'mental process' at all! – For that is the way of talking which confuses you. Instead, ask yourself: in what sort of case, in what kind of circumstances, do we say, 'Now I know how to go on'? I mean, if the formula has occurred to me.
>
> . . .
>
> In the sense in which there are processes (including mental processes) which are characteristic of understanding, understanding is not a mental process. (*PI* I, §§ 153–4)

Whatever experiences tend to accompany suddenly understanding this or that, they would at most be symptomatic of understanding, not criterial. The point of Wittgenstein's enigmatic remark, 'An "inner process" stands in need of outward criteria' (*PI* I, § 580), should perhaps be sought for in this context.[29]

---

[29] John Hunter points to some serious difficulties about the reading of this remark. See his 'Wittgenstein on Inner Processes and Outward Criteria', 805–17. Along similar lines, P. M. S. Hacker remarks: 'This is not a statement of a fundamental (grammatical) principle, but an ironic one – ironic, because believing is *not* an inner process' (the remark occurring in the context of a discussion about belief). Hacker, *Wittgenstein: Mind and Will*, 463. Also, compare Hanfling, 'Criteria', 45.

Later on, Wittgenstein considers the question, 'What happens when a man suddenly understands?' And he responds:

> The question is badly framed. If it is a question about the meaning of the expression 'sudden understanding', the answer is not pointing to a process to which we give this name. – The question might mean: what are the symptoms of sudden understanding; what are its characteristic mental accompaniments? . . .
>
> The question what the expression means is not answered by such a description; and this tempts us to conclude that understanding is a specific indefinable experience.
>
> But one forgets that the question which should be our concern is: how do we *compare* these experiences; what criterion of identity *do we stipulate* for their occurrence? (*PI* I, §§ 321–2)

Since no specific description of an experience would seem to have the characteristics requisite for considering it an experience of understanding, we are tempted to assume that the experience in question is indefinable (i.e. it has no character apart from being the experience of sudden understanding). But once that assumption is made, the experience ceases to perform the task for which it was postulated: to inform us that we have understood. It cannot perform that task if we have to be aware that we have understood in order to identify it as the relevant experience.

Whence the attraction of the idea that, if a person is to be in a position to tell that he knows how to play chess or that he understands how to continue a number series, there must be a specific inner experience that tips him off? I would suggest that it derives from an inclination to regard observation statements as the paradigm of the intentional use of language. It may seem natural to assume that, if I am to be in a position to assert that something is the case, there must be something present to my senses or present in my mind from which I may, as it were, 'read off' what is the case.

However, even if there were a typical experience accompanying my coming to understand this or that, the experience could not be identified with the understanding itself: whether or not I understood would depend on how I went on to perform. The word 'must' in the last sentence of the previous paragraph – as in many cases in which Wittgenstein uses the word – should warn us that we are here tempted to formulate an a priori requirement. Reflection should make it clear that some specific experience warranting a person's claim to understand this or that has no place in our actual practices of testing a person's understanding, of helping her understand something or other. It is simply a fact that people do acquire the ability to acknowledge that they have come to understand something, that they know how to play chess, that they are reading, and so on. Doing so does not involve relying on criteria (talk which does not involve criteria will be the theme of the Section 1.3). How a child *acquires* the ability to acknowledge that she understands something, on the other hand, is perhaps a question for psychology – it is not to be resolved a priori.

We might say: the use of words to talk about understanding (as well as about knowledge, thought, intention, feelings, etc.) is dependent on the existence of an alignment between first person uses of these words on the one hand and their second and third person uses on the other hand. By an alignment, I mean the fact that people learn to use such words in the first person in a way that fits in with the way the words are used in speaking to them or about them: thus, in a great many cases in which a person will claim to have understood something, others will agree that she did indeed understand it, and vice versa; and where such agreement is not reached, we will normally find ways of accounting for the discrepancy. The attempt to find an explanation of these alignments in terms of specific experiences is doomed to failure, since the relation between any given experiences and the corresponding actions is contingent. In fact, the notion that there must be some general explanation of that alignment is vain, for it is the actual variety of ways in which these words are used that shapes what understanding, knowledge, intention, and so on are – and hence defines what it is for the uses of those respective words to *be in alignment*.

Consideration of the criteria of understanding helps bring attention to another important point. Many readers of Wittgenstein have tended to regard criteria as bound up with *words* in the language, rather like definitions which might be listed in a dictionary. Where the technical terms of some profession or discipline are concerned, this may be a plausible conception. However, when we think of many of the words that are an object of special attention in *Philosophical Investigations*, words such as 'understand', for instance, with their widely ramified uses, it hardly makes sense to try to formulate criteria for their use in general terms. Thus, the criterion for having understood a number series is different from the criterion of having understood a road sign, or the doctor's advice, or something spoken in Italian, or a person, or a piano sonata, and so on. Because of this, it is more fruitful to think of the question of the criteria of understanding as arising in relation to given conversational contexts rather than with regard to the word itself. Similar considerations apply to many of the other words we apply to human thought and action, such as 'know', or 'remember', or 'intend', or 'believe', or 'want', or 'attend'.

## 1.3 No Criteria

As with understanding, there is a temptation to take it for granted that first person utterances about sensations must be grounded in our ability to recognize specific experiences – what I feel is my criterion of having this or that sensation. However, in *PI* I, § 290, Wittgenstein writes: 'It is not, of course, that I identify my sensation by means of criteria; it is rather that I use the same expression. But it is not as if the language-game *ends* with this; it begins with this'.

In other words, if I have a pain in my thumb, I do not rely on criteria to decide that it is a pain I feel. On what basis do we say this? Is it an empirical observation? It is, rather, a remark on how we normally talk about pain. When someone wants to find out how it is with me, one of the things she will do is ask me how I feel. In normal circumstances, however, she will not ask me whether I'm sure what I claim to feel is really pain. (She might ask that if I were just learning to speak English.) In the ordinary language-game of talking about pain, a person's being in a position to say whether she is in pain or not is not questioned.

In *PI* I, § 288, Wittgenstein writes

> If someone said 'I don't know if what I have is a pain or something else', we would think, perhaps, that he does not know what the English word 'pain' means; and we'd explain it to him. – How? Perhaps by means of gestures, or by pricking him with a pin and saying: 'See, that's pain!' This explanation of a word, like any other, he might understand right, wrong, or not at all. And he will show which by his use of the word, in this as in other cases.
>
> If he now said, for example: 'Oh, I know what "pain" means; what I don't know is whether this, that I have now, is pain' – we'd merely shake our heads and have to regard his words as a strange reaction which we can't make anything of.

In *PI* I, § 244, Wittgenstein asks:

> How do words refer to sensations? – There doesn't seem to be any problem here; don't we talk about sensations every day, and name them? But how is the connection between the name and the thing named set up? This question is the same as: how does a human being learn the meaning of names of sensations? For example, of the word 'pain'. Here is one possibility: words are connected with the primitive, natural, expressions of sensation and used in their place. A child has hurt himself and he cries; and then adults talk to him and teach him exclamations and, later, sentences. They teach the child new pain-behaviour.
>
> 'So you are saying that the word "pain" really means crying?' – On the contrary: the verbal expression of pain replaces crying and does not describe it.

And in § 245: 'How can I even attempt to interpose language between the expression of pain and the pain?'

The learner does strive to get from her natural expression of pain to the verbal expression. When he comes to speak of himself as being in pain, his doing so is no more based on his *recognizing* that this is pain than his earlier crying out was – nor does he observe and learn to recognize his own *expressions* of pain. In trying to grasp the situation of learning, we should focus on the role of the second person: it is the teacher (say, the parent) who recognizes, from the child's expressions – as well as, in most cases, from the circumstances – that he is in pain, and provides him with the verbal expression (often in connection with expressing pity or concern). The learner's fulfilling the conditions of having learnt verbal expressions of pain is judged by the other (exactly how the learning process takes place in the child, on the other hand, is a question for child psychology).

See also *PI* I, §271:

> 'Imagine a person who could not remember what the word "pain" meant – so that he constantly called different things by that name – but nevertheless used it in accordance with the usual symptoms and presuppositions of pain' – in short, he uses it as we all do. Here I'd like to say: a wheel that can be turned though nothing else moves with it is not part of the mechanism.

And the end of *PI* I, § 288: 'My temptation to say that one might take a sensation for something other than what it is arises from this: if I assume the abrogation of the normal language-game with the expression of a sensation, I need a criterion of identity for the sensation; and then the possibility of error also exists.'

That is, if I ignore the normal practice of expressing sensations, it will seem I need a criterion for deciding whether what I am feeling is pain or not. In *PI* I, § 304, Wittgenstein suggests that we should reject 'the grammar which tends to force itself on us here'; in other words, we should 'make a radical break with the idea that language always functions in one way, always serves the same purpose: to convey thoughts – which may be about houses, pains, good and evil, or whatever'.

By looking at the practice of pain talk, we will recognize that when I express my pain, my words have a different relation to their object than, say, when I describe the exterior of a house.

Thus, it is important to take note of the division of roles between the first person and the second and third person that characterizes the everyday practice of speaking about sensations. Something similar is to be said about talk about intentions, beliefs, wishes, and so on, although in the case of some of these words there is a variety of practices. An expression of belief is normally a guarded judgment, rather than a report about my inner state based on self-observation. If I say, 'I *believe* that's Joe's car' (say, while we are waiting impatiently for Joe to pick us up), I'm telling my company to get ready to jump in, rather than informing them of how things stand with me. If someone asks me,

'Are you sure?' he will not be taken to be asking whether I am sure that is what I believe, but how certain my surmise is. However, the expression 'I believe . . . ' can also be used in a confessional way, as when someone says 'I know she's dead but it seems as if I don't really believe it'. Here, it appears, it is a *report*, maybe partly based on my observing my expectations and reactions. This use of the word 'believe' is obviously secondary to its use in making guarded judg-ments. In these secondary uses, the speaker might in some cases rely on criteria, as in 'I must have believed I would get the job since I was quite taken aback when I found out I did not.'

## 2 Practices

### 2.1 Practices in *Philosophical Investigations*

I have suggested that when Wittgenstein talks about criterial claims, in most cases it is fruitful to think about them as employed in the description of a practice, rather than as providing a general description of the way some word is used in the language. To some extent, then, criteria and practices go together in Wittgenstein's thinking. (As will be discussed in Section 5.2, in some cases criterial claims do not belong to the description of a practice but are rather to be thought of as having application in particular cases.)

What, then, does Wittgenstein mean by the word 'practice'? I would suggest that he does not employ the word as a technical term, rather he relies on our familiarity with the word from everyday contexts.

There are about 100 occurrences of the word 'practice' (German '*Praxis*') in the *Nachlass*. The earliest occurrences are from 1931.

In *Philosophical Investigations*, the word 'practice' occurs only five times. In I § 7, in describing a way of using language, Wittgenstein talks of the practice of the use of language. In I § 21 he talks about a form of words having the function of a command in a linguistic practice; in I § 51 he talks about certain elements corresponding to the signs in the practice of a language; in I § 197 he talks of the playing of chess as a practice; and in I § 202 he says that following a rule is a practice.

In addition, in I § 54, at Wittgenstein's behest, the translation of *aus der Praxis des Spiels'*, which Rhees had rendered as 'from the practice of the game' in his unpublished translation, was changed into 'from the way the game is played' (the whole sentence is: 'But we say that it is played according to such-and-such rules because an observer can read these rules off from the way the game is played – like a natural law governing the play').[30] In fact, this correction

---

[30] See Hacker & Schulte, 'Endnotes', 247. This remark is discussed in Section 2.3.

gives an indication of how the word 'practice' is to be understood: a practice is, simply, a way things are (customarily) done. Examples of this are various customary activities: greeting, preparing and eating a meal, performing a ritual, using road signs, harvesting crops, teaching a class, washing one's hands, singing in a choir, running a university, sewing on buttons, making a bed, telling a story, getting dressed and undressed, doing an experiment in chemistry, starting a war, getting married, shovelling snow, doing a calculation in arithmetic, consoling a child who has hurt herself, and so on. Practices may be carried out individually or collaboratively, they may be shared by a limited group (e.g. a family), they may be local, common to a culture, or global.

The word 'practice' is closely connected with the words 'language-game', 'rule-following', and 'custom' as they occur in *Philosophical Investigations*. Wittgenstein gives an account of a practice in *Philosophical Investigations*, in what has become known as the builders' language-game (*PI* I, § 2): A is building something and B has been taught to bring him the building stones he calls for: 'block', 'pillar', 'slab', 'beam'. The word 'language-game' is introduced in I § 7:

> In the practice of the use of language (2) [the language of the builders] one party calls out the words, the other acts on them. However, in instruction in the language the following process will occur: the learner names the objects; that is, he utters the word when the teacher points at the stone. – Indeed, there will be an even simpler exercise: the pupil repeats the words after the teacher – both of these being language-like processes.
>
> We can also think of the whole process of using words in (2) as one of those games by means of which children learn their native language. I will call these games 'language-games' and will sometimes speak of a primitive language as a language-game.
>
> And the processes of naming the stones and of repeating words after someone might also be called language-games. Think of certain uses that are made of words in games like ring-a-ring-a-roses.
>
> *I shall also call the whole, consisting of language and the activities into which it is woven, a 'language-game.'* (My italics.)

## 2.2 A Practice Is a Recurrent Way of Acting

A practice consists in a way in which individuals or groups of people will customarily act in certain situations or carry out certain activities. In *PI* I, § 199, Wittgenstein writes:

> Is what we call 'following a rule' something that it would be possible for only one man, only once in a lifetime, to do? – And this is, of course, a gloss on the grammar of the expression 'to follow a rule'.

> It is not possible that there should have been only one occasion on which
> only one person followed a rule. It is not possible that there should have been
> only one occasion on which a report was made, an order given or understood;
> and so on. – To follow a rule, to make a report, to give an order, to play a game
> of chess are customs (usages, institutions).[31]

## 2.3 Practice and Criticism

A practice involves the notion that one may go wrong in carrying out (or
attempting to carry out) the activity in question. Those who participate in the
practice may criticize each other's performance – often by appealing to the
customary way of proceeding. (The right way of going on may, however, be
a matter of contention.)

To speak of a practice, in other words, is not to speak of a natural law of
human behaviour. Nor is it simply an ideal of behaviour. To participate in
a practice is to mostly conform to it.

Another way of putting this is to say that the word 'practice' is closely
connected with the idea of rule-following. There has been a large discussion
of rules and rule-following in the literature on Wittgenstein's philosophy. I do
not wish to go into that discussion here. In any case, we should note that there is
a degree of openness in the way Wittgenstein thinks about the relation between
rules and practices, as made clear in *PI* I, § 54:

> Just think of the kinds of case where we say that a game is played according to
> a particular rule.
>    The rule may be an aid in teaching the game. The learner is told it and
> given practice in applying it. – Or it is a tool of the game itself. – Or a rule is
> employed neither in the teaching nor in the game itself; nor is it set down in
> a list of rules. One learns the game by watching how others play it. But we say
> that it is played according to such-and-such rules because an observer can
> read these rules off from the way the game is played – like a natural law
> governing the play. – But how does the observer distinguish in this case
> between players' mistakes and correct play? – There are characteristic signs
> of it in the players' behaviour. Think of the behaviour characteristic of
> someone correcting a slip of the tongue. It would be possible to recognize
> that someone was doing so even without knowing his language.

---

[31] Cp. *PI* I, § 204: 'As things are, I can, for example, invent a game that is never played by anyone. –
But would the following be possible too: mankind has never played any games; once though,
someone invented a game – which, however, was never played?'
   Obviously, Wittgenstein is suggesting that this notion is absurd. One might ask: what would
the act of inventing the game consist in? If there are no earlier games to which the inventor can
relate his invention, and neither is his invention ever put into practice, wherein would his having
invented a game consist?

Thus, in some cases, the rule formulation enters into the teaching or the playing of the game. (I guess the football referee signalling what rule had been violated when stopping play would be an instance of the latter.) The players are thinking of what they are doing in terms of the following of rules. But it is important to note that a game may be said to be played – or some other practice be carried out – according to rules without any rule ever being formulated by the participants. In this case, the rule may be formulated by an observer: this is how things are usually done. Maybe one could say, 'It is as if they followed such and such a rule.' However, Wittgenstein's formulation 'like a natural law governing the play' is liable to be misunderstood. For, as he goes on to point out, in order to formulate the rule, an observer should be able to tell mistakes apart from cases in which the players are proceeding correctly. In relation to natural laws, on the other hand, there are of course no 'mistakes'.

The basic point is that, within a practice, there is room for criticism and defence against criticism, whether or not there are also formulated rules, or rules that an observer might detect, or nothing rule-like. It is important to note the latter possibility: for instance, there is no non-circular way of giving rules for the application of colour-words. Similarly, when it comes to grammar or (English) spelling, for instance, there are cases in which the distinction between correct and incorrect is upheld but it would not be possible to formulate any general rules.

Even with formulated rules, it is important to note that the actual playing of the game is, in an important sense, logically prior to the rule formulations: the practice shows what it is to follow the rule. It would be an error to think of the rule formulation as a kind of premise, a foundation, from which the practice is derived; rather, where rules are formulated, the formulated rules are *part* of the practice. This may be Wittgenstein's point in saying, in *PI* I, §202, 'following a rule is a practice' – not the other way round.

Of course, one could imagine someone inaugurating a game by formulating a set of rules – but in that case, he would be relying on a familiarity with other games and rule formulations. This is connected with an important point about the way we may speak about practices: there is no determinate way of delimiting practices, rather practices may be conceived more or less comprehensively. Thus, team sports, or ball games, or association football might in a given context be mentioned as examples of a practice. And one practice may gradually shade into another without any sharp lines of distinction.

In *PI* I, § 83, Wittgenstein writes:

> We can easily imagine people amusing themselves in a field by playing with
> a ball like this: starting various existing games, but playing several without

finishing them, and in between throwing the ball aimlessly into the air, chasing one another with the ball, throwing it at one another for a joke, and so on. And now someone says: The whole time they are playing a ball-game and therefore are following definite rules at every throw.

And is there not also the case where we play, and make up the rules as we go along? And even where we alter them – as we go along.

Similarly, we can think of various practices arising, being transformed or combined, branching out in different directions, and of disagreements arising and being negotiated or conflicts being found irreconcilable, and so on.

In *PI* I, § 202, after writing '"following a rule" is a practice', Wittgenstein goes on: 'And to think one is following a rule is not to follow a rule. And that's why it is not possible to follow a rule "privately": otherwise thinking one was following a rule would be the same thing as following it.'

## 2.4 Practices Are Shared

The practices we have mentioned here are shared by several participants. Could there also be solitary practices? We might observe the customary behaviour of an individual living by herself, let's call her Sarah. We see her lock the door and hide the key, or we see her gathering wood and starting a fire. These activities are familiar from the lives we share with other people and it may be natural for us to describe her actions accordingly. But she might also regularly be behaving in unfamiliar ways, and we might be unable to see the point of that behaviour. There would be no one to correct her, so we have no way of distinguishing between her following the practice correctly or deviating from it. In that case, we would not see Sarah's behaviour under an aspect of rule-following. Could we still call it a practice? I guess the answer to that question is a matter of taste; only we should be clear that if we use the word here its use differs from the case in which we talk about *shared* practices.

G. P. Baker and P. M. S. Hacker, in a presentation of Wittgenstein's discussion of criteria which is, on the whole, illuminating, downplay the importance of sharing for the application of criteria of correctness. They write:

> Since mastery of a technique is exhibited in acts which satisfy the criteria of correctness internal to the technique . . ., this manifestly guarantees the possibility of distinguishing between a person's thinking that he is following a rule and his actually doing so. It is, however, tempting to construct an explanation for the objectivity by reference to the idea that techniques are inherently *social*. On such an interpretation, 'correct' . . . would be defined or explained by reference to what most qualified members of a practice do from case to case.[32]

---

[32] Baker & Hacker, *Wittgenstein: Rules, Grammar and Necessity*, 164.

They call this a 'radically mistaken' account, on the grounds that 'any definition of "correct" in terms of consensus or statistical regularity treats correctness as externally related to the technique of applying a given rule, whereas stipulating criteria of correctness is an essential part of explaining any rule whatever.'[33]

Now, this is an important point as far as it goes. But it fails to grasp the sense in which criteria of correctness are internal to a practice. When it is claimed that there may be an application for the correct/incorrect distinction in a practice to the extent that the practice is shared by several participants, this claim does not presuppose that there must be a procedure for deciding once and for all (say, by invoking 'consensus or statistical regularity') which ways of proceeding are correct. Rather, there is an application for the distinction in as far as those who *participate* in the practice will use it, for instance, in correcting one another. It is possible, of course, that the participants will be unable to agree on what is correct.[34]

## 2.5 Games and Other Practices

As we have seen, Wittgenstein often uses (competitive) games as a model in discussing practices. (This also extends to his use of the game metaphor in talking about various uses of language.) Considered as practices, games possess a number of peculiarities: this may be the reason we do not normally refer to games as practices. Let us consider the place games normally hold in *our* culture, without making any cross-cultural claims. Games usually constitute limited wholes that are easy to survey, often involving a limited set of clearly formulated rules through which the participants in the game consciously identify their actions. Many other practices do not have sharply defined limits: if there are rules, they may be fleeting, and there are often individual variations in the way people consider it correct to proceed within a practice. While games, in many cases, are intentionally instituted, many practices arise and change spontaneously. Unlike what is the case with a large number of other practices, participation in a game is usually undertaken consciously and voluntarily. Thus, while there is no rule of football stipulating that anyone has to play football, the case is different with many other practices: in being taught politeness, for instance, one is not simply taught how to be polite, but also that one *ought* to be polite. Furthermore, in competitive games, the importance of individual moves is constituted by their contributing to the aim of winning the

---

[33] Ibid.
[34] I have discussed this issue in 'The Need for a Listener and Community Standards', 73–86, esp. 82–6.

game; how winning is defined, on the other hand, is in a sense arbitrary. The importance of playing is bestowed on the game by players themselves and onlookers, it does not primarily derive from any external concerns (though they may, of course, come to play a role). Some practices are instrumental, that is, the correct way of proceeding, wholly or in part, is dependent on the agents' success in achieving some result. In the case of many other practices, an activity is judged by criteria that are internal to the practice (singing a song, greeting someone, carrying out a ritual), though their importance may be bound up with other concerns. Competitive games on their part, we might say, have an instrumentality that is internal to the game.

On the distinction between practices governed by external and internal criteria, Wittgenstein writes:

> Why don't I call cookery rules arbitrary, and why am I tempted to call the rules of grammar arbitrary? Because 'cookery' is defined by its end, whereas 'speaking' is not. That is why the use of language is in a sense autonomous, as cooking and washing are not. You cook badly if you are guided in your cooking by rules other than the right ones; but if you follow other rules than those of chess you are *playing another game*; and if you follow grammatical rules other than such-and-such ones, that does not mean you say something wrong, no, you are speaking of something else.[35]

This remark is actually somewhat problematic (which may account for Wittgenstein's not having included it in *Philosophical Investigations*). On the one hand, the distinction between autonomous practices and practices guided by external purposes is not so sharp as Wittgenstein makes it out to be; on the other hand, even in the case of an autonomous practice, I may *of course* be criticized for not following the rules that are relevant to the interaction in which I am involved.

In any case, the clearly circumscribed character which is typical of games explains their usefulness as models of human practices, but at the same time that is precisely the feature that makes their use as models risky, in tempting us to overlook the variety and complexity of human practices. This is a risk that should constantly be kept in mind when practices are considered under the model of games. (This is true not least of the concept of a language-game.[36])

## 2.6 A Practice as a Logical Space

A practice provides a logical space for the application of certain words. Thus, it is in the context of a certain practice that there will be such a thing as a road sign

---

[35] Wittgenstein, *Zettel*, § 320.
[36] These risks are well brought out in Rhees, 'Wittgenstein's Builders', 178–97.

and such a thing as following (or failing to follow) a road sign (see *PI* I, § 198). Similarly, in a game of chess there will be such a thing as checkmating your opponent, in football there will be offsides and goals; actions such as greetings, apologies, promises, commands, requests, reports, confessions, and so on are part of practices. Only within a (shared) practice will there be such a thing as following rules. Being taught a practice makes me capable of carrying out certain activities – and in another sense, the existence of the practice makes doing those things possible for me.[37] It also makes it possible to attribute certain intentions to me. Thus, I can decide to play a game of chess because there is such a practice, and because I have learnt it. In *PI* I, § 197, Wittgenstein writes: 'Where is the connection effected between the sense of the words "Let's play a game of chess" and all the rules of the game? – Well, in the list of rules of the game, in the teaching of it, in the everyday practice of playing.'

For a time, on a widely accepted reading of Wittgenstein's later philosophy, criteria offered a definition of (or a definition-like assertion about) the meaning of many of the words in the language. As I shall be arguing later, this is a misunderstanding which primarily grew out of a misleading formulation by Wittgenstein in *The Blue Book*. Against this, it is my contention that for Wittgenstein criteria have a role in the context of characterizing practices, whether in accounting for some actual human practice, in imagining some conceivable practice, or in testing the viability of some proposed practice. One and the same word (say, 'understand', 'know', 'win') may enter into a variety of practices, the relevant criterion varying with the practice. In indicating the criterion for some claim, we are trying to clarify how certain crucial decisions are made within the practice. Criteria could be said to be part of the limits of a practice: thus, while there is a huge number of possible ways the pieces may be arranged on the board, certain positions will always constitute checkmate.

Of course, our language contains many technical terms, say, of science, mathematics, or law, the use of which is exclusively or very largely confined to some specific practice, and, in their case, definition and criterion may be taken to coincide. However, a great many words of our language – and this is true, in particular, of the words which philosophical bewilderment tends to circle around – recur in various practices, and it is important to realize that those words, taken by themselves, are not sufficient to identify a *single* practice.

---

[37] *PI* I, § 260: 'Then did the man who made the entry in the calendar make a note of nothing whatever? – Don't consider it a matter of course that a person is making a note of something when he makes a mark – say in a calendar. For a note has a function, and this "S" so far has none.' Compare *PI* I, § 258.

Our overlooking this point, is, I think, responsible for many of the issues that are taken to be problematic in philosophy.

## 3 *The Blue Book*: The Case of Angina

While the word 'criterion' occurs frequently in Wittgenstein's manuscripts from 1929 onward, the one occasion in which he proposes something like a definition of the word is in what has become known as *The Blue Book* (which was actually a dictation to his class in Cambridge, 1933–4). He says:

> Let us introduce two antithetical terms in order to avoid certain elementary confusions: To the question 'How do you know that so-and-so is the case?', we sometimes answer by giving "*criteria*" and sometimes by giving "*symptoms*". If medical science calls angina an inflammation caused by a particular bacillus, and we ask in a particular case 'why do you say this man has got angina?' then the answer 'I have found the bacillus so-and-so in his blood' gives us the criterion, or what we may call the defining criterion of angina. If on the other hand the answer was, 'His throat is inflamed', this might give us a symptom of angina. I call 'symptom' a phenomenon of which experience has taught us that it coincided, in some way or other, with the phenomenon which is our defining criterion. Then to say, 'A man has angina whenever he has an inflamed throat' is to make a hypothesis. (24–5)

A brief lexical note may be in order here. The example Wittgenstein has in mind is evidently what in English is usually called a strep throat (*streptococcal pharyngitis*), and which is called *Angina* in German (and Swedish). This condition is caused by a strain of streptococci (not bacilli). In English, the word 'angina', on the other hand, is normally short for *angina pectoris*, a heart condition.[38]

Let us consider how we normally talk about symptoms and diagnoses. We commonly distinguish between the 'symptoms' of a disease and the 'disease' itself. Symptoms are often non-specific: one and the same condition may be a symptom of several different diseases. Sometimes what could be a symptom of a disease (e.g. fatigue) may leave it open whether a person is actually *ill*. When Wittgenstein asks, 'How do you know that so-and-so is the case?', in this connection, he may have two questions in mind. One is the question, 'How does one know that the patient is really ill?' This will often enough be evident from the symptoms; in fact, if it were not for some of the symptoms, the disease would not really bother us (except because of the development it may forebode, say, in terms of symptoms that may be expected to develop later on). The other

---

[38]  As Rogers Albritton points out, the presence of a certain strand of bacteria would not by itself be grounds for a diagnosis of angina, rather, the illness is only present when those bacteria actually cause an inflammation. Albritton, 'On Wittgenstein's Use', 234, note 4.

question is, 'How do you know she suffers from this particular disease?' Here, again, symptoms may yield the answer, if they are specific enough. Indeed, when it comes to mental illness, there is usually nothing to go by except symptoms – the symptoms, we might say, *are* the illness. (This is also true of some somatic conditions such as migraine.)

In the context of normal conversation, one reason it may be important to single out certain aspects of a person's condition – say, the presence of strepto-cocci in her throat or bloodstream – and to contrast them with the symptoms of the disease is because it provides us with the *cause* of the disease, which in turn may give us a clue to how it is to be treated, or what the prognosis is – or how others may avoid it. Here, though, we would not normally talk about *criteria*.

On the other hand, talk of criteria might be relevant in some types of medical research. In the case of an epidemic, it may be important to establish how far it has spread, and accordingly we may wish to distinguish cases of one particular infection from other cases displaying similar symptoms. Here there is a statistical interest in distinguishing cases by criteria. Along the same lines, a publication like *Diagnostic and Statistical Manual of Mental Disorders*, issued by the American Psychiatric Association, proposes criteria for identify-ing various forms of mental illness, but here the criteria for the most part are what we would call symptoms.

In short, the distinction criteria–symptoms as introduced by Wittgenstein does not seem to answer to familiar ways of talking about symptoms and diseases. It is in fact somewhat confusing to use medical discourse as a model for what Wittgenstein means to be talking about. I wish to argue – and it appears to be widely held – that this passage is misleading if read as a gateway to Wittgenstein's use of the word 'criterion' in his later work. Nevertheless, that was the role it was given in much of the early debate about criteria.[39]

## 4 The Post-Wittgensteinian Debate

In what follows, I wish to give an overview of parts of the debate to which Wittgenstein's use of 'criteria' gave rise. The debate has two points of focus – which are, however, closely connected with one another. On the one hand, it concerns the question of what light Wittgensteinian criteria might be taken to throw on issues in the philosophy of language. Wittgenstein's use of criteria has been taken to pose a challenge to what was for long the received view: the idea that the only kind of logical or conceptual connection between statements is a deductive relation, in other

---

[39] In fact, as will be spelled out later on, according to John Cook this passage is not to be taken to express Wittgenstein's own view, but rather a view he is setting up for criticism.

words that the only type of logical relation (meaning relation) between statements is either one of entailment or one of contradiction. The debate has been constituted by various attempts to accommodate criterial relations that are conceptual but not deductive.

The second important point of focus has been the other-minds problem. A perennial conundrum in philosophy concerns our ability to know another's mind. The other-minds skeptic argues that the mind of another is inaccessible, our only access is to the other's body and its movements on the basis of which we may construct more or less uncertain conjectures about her thoughts, feelings, sensations, and so on. Some have argued that the consideration of Wittgensteinian criteria shows that the starting point for the other-minds problem as it is envisaged by the skeptic is not coherent. Others have argued that Wittgenstein's primary concern in discussing the criteria of psychological statements is with the description of uses of language rather than with combatting skepticism.

In what follows, I will give a short overview of some of the main contributions to the debate about criteria which followed the publication of *Philosophical Investigations*.

## 4.1 Norman Malcolm: Defining Criterion

In 1954, Wittgenstein's student Norman Malcolm published an influential review of Wittgenstein's *Philosophical Investigations*. This lucid text was one of the first reading guides to Wittgenstein's work. The short section on criteria (6 pages) in this review, I believe, had a powerful influence on the ensuing debate about criteria.

Malcolm starts out by saying: 'It is with some reluctance I will undertake to say a little bit about his notion of a "criterion", a most difficult region in Wittgenstein's philosophy' (83). He then goes on to connect criteria with the learning of words:

> If you have succeeded in bringing to mind what it is that would show that [the learner] *grasped* your teaching, that he *understood* the use of the words, then you have elicited the 'criterion' for their use.... Wittgenstein exhorts us, over and over, to bethink ourselves of how we learned to use this or that form of words or of how we should teach it to a child. The purpose of this ... is to bring into view those features of someone's circumstances and behavior that *settle* the question of whether the words (e.g. 'He is calculating in his head') rightly apply to him. Those features constitute the 'criterion' of calculating in one's head.... To undertake to describe this may be called a 'logical' investigation. (83–4)

As Malcolm makes clear, what he is envisaging is not a psychological inquiry into the learning processes themselves. The emphasis is on how we can tell whether the processes of teaching and learning have been successful. The suggestion that one way of getting clear about what we mean by a word is by reflecting on what would show that someone had understood the word correctly – in other words, on the criteria of understanding – is a useful one: as Malcolm points out, it brings the inquiry down to earth. It is a way of reminding ourselves of concrete contexts in which a word is used, in contrast to our inclination, in doing philosophy, to contemplate words in isolation from their place in the stream of life.[40]

The view formulated by Malcolm has come to be known as the *'defining criteria' view*: 'that so-and-so is the criterion of *y* is a matter, not of experience, but of definition. The satisfaction of the criterion of *y* establishes the existence of *y* beyond question' (84). However, Malcolm points out, the propositions that describe the criterion of someone's being in pain do not *entail* the proposition 'He is in pain'. 'A criterion is satisfied *only in certain circumstances'* – not, for instance, if the person is play-acting, simulating pain, and so on. Nor can one establish an entailment by ruling out all the conceivable countervailing factors, since the list of those factors is open-ended (85–6).

Malcolm then addresses the question how we can ever be certain that someone is in pain if this does not follow logically from his behaviour and the circumstances. How can we exclude the possibility that he is pretending? He points out that there are many situations in real life where a doubt simply would not arise:

> What we sometimes do is draw a boundary around *this* behavior in *these* circumstances and say 'Any additional circumstances that might come to light will be irrelevant to whether this man is in pain.'[41] ... [I]f someone *always* had endless doubts about the genuineness of expressions of pain, it would mean that he was not using *any criterion* of another's being in pain.... It is senseless to suppose that he has this concept [the concept of pain] and yet always doubts. (87–9)

There is a detailed working out of a conception much along the same lines, in John Canfield's book *Wittgenstein: Language and World*.[42]

## 4.2 Noninductive Evidence

The so-called noninductive evidence view has been advanced as an alternative to the defining criterion view. The term 'noninductive evidence' was coined by Malcolm's colleague Sydney Shoemaker. In his words,

---

[40] Compare Wittgenstein, *Zettel*, § 173.
[41] Or rather maybe we simply do not take seriously the possibility that any more circumstances relevant to this man's being in pain *will* come to light.
[42] Canfield, *Wittgenstein: Language and World* (1981).

> For present purposes we may characterize the criteria for the truth of a judgment as those states of affairs that are (whose existence would be) direct and noninductive evidence in favor of the truth of the judgment. A test of whether something is one of the criteria for the truth of judgments of a certain kind is whether it is conceivable that we might discover empirically that it is not, or has ceased to be, evidence in favor of the truth of such judgments. If it is evidence, and it is not conceivable that that it could be discovered not to be (or no longer to be) evidence, then it is one of the criteria.[43]

Or, as summarized by Canfield (who is critical of this position): on this view, *C* is the criterion for *S* means, 'It is necessarily true that *C* is evidence for *S*' (81). A criterion, on this reading, is a method for establishing that something is so – as when, for instance, establishing that someone holds a certain opinion by hearing her express that opinion – where the validity of the method is not contingent on empirical observation (our having discovered that people tend to express the opinions they hold) but is determined by the meaning of the phrase 'to hold an opinion'. Nevertheless, on this view, the method is not fail-safe. As was said, people may pretend to hold opinions they do not hold, or they may speak ironically, or their expression may misfire because they are under a misapprehension concerning the meaning of some term, or they may have an incomplete grasp of the issue at stake, or the like. Nor would it be possible to list all the conditions of this kind under which the method will not be reliable.[44] So, while it is a point of grammar that what someone says is 'necessarily' a ground for attributing an opinion to him, it is not a conclusive ground; the criterion being fulfilled does not entail that the statement is true. This point is often expressed by saying that the criterion is defeasible.

A view which has similarities both to the defining criterion view and the noninductive evidence view is advanced in Rogers Albritton's classical essay, 'On Wittgenstein's Use of the Term "Criterion"'. According to Albritton (whose commentary is mainly, though not exclusively, based on *The Blue and Brown Books*, and whose discussion centres around the question of the criteria for toothache), the criterion for something being so is a logically necessary and sufficient criterion for its being so. As I understand him, the assertions 'If the criteria of A's having toothache are satisfied then he has toothache', and 'If A has toothache the criteria for his having toothache are satisfied' are tautologies. However, he says, if in place of 'criteria for having toothache' we

---

[43] In his book *Self-Knowledge and Self-Identity*, 3–4. Similar views have been held by, among others, Kenny, 'Criterion', and Baker, 'Criteria'.

[44] What will be taken to show a person's (true) opinion will also vary depending on the situation at hand, say, between the case of taking an opinion poll and the case in which I have a serious discussion with a friend concerning a controversial issue.

substitute a description of the criterion such as 'a man sits rocking miserably back and forth, holding his jaw, every now and then cautiously pushing at a loose tooth on that side with certain kinds of grimaces and sharp intakes of breath', then, while in normal circumstances I would be justified in saying that he has a toothache, it does not necessarily follow that he does. (In a postscript from 1966, he abandons the view that criterial claims constitute necessary truths.[45])

I shall get back to the debate between those who hold the defining criteria view and those who hold the noninductive evidence view in Section 5.2.

## 4.3 John Cook

John Cook, in his inspiring essay 'Human Beings', rejects the idea that Wittgenstein introduced talk about criteria as a means of solving the problem of our knowledge of other minds.[46] Rather, he argues, Wittgenstein's purpose was to criticize a view of language. In introducing the notion of a defining criterion in *The Blue Book* passage we quoted earlier, Cook maintains, Wittgenstein was actually formulating an idea he meant to criticize. This is the idea that all the instances to which a general term applies must have something in common – the idea that there is a 'law in the way a word is used'.[47] This alleged common element, Cook proposes, might be called 'the defining criterion'. (The conception Cook criticizes here is apparently that echoed in Canfield's formulation: 'If the defining criterion view is correct, then the criterial relation is a depth grammatical or logical one; that is, it holds in virtue of a rule of language.'[48]) On this view, when it comes to the question whether a term applies, then whatever else may be true of the case, apart from this defining criterion, is at most indirectly relevant. Such other things may be called 'symptoms'. There should, accordingly, be a defining criterion for words like 'expectation' and 'knowledge': when we ask 'What is expecting?' and consider various cases, the varying details are to be dismissed as irrelevant to the question. Only what the cases have in common could be relevant for clarifying what expecting is. However, Cook argues, this way of stating the issue is incoherent. If the defining criterion is what makes these cases instances of expecting, and we have yet to find out what that criterion is, how can we know that they are all cases of expecting? It seems, Cook argues, we have to conclude either that we cannot know, or that our knowing that

---

[45] Albritton, 'On Wittgenstein's Use', 247–59.
[46] Winch (ed.), *Studies in the Philosophy of Wittgenstein*, 117–51. The relevant passage is on pp. 133–5.
[47] Wittgenstein, *The Blue Book*, 27.    [48] Canfield, *Wittgenstein: Language and World*, 87.

something is a case of expecting is not dependent on our identifying a common element.

In this connection, Cook suggests, we may consider Wittgenstein's remark, *Philosophical Investigations*, I § 164, about the idea that in reading we *derive* the spoken from the printed words (as suggested in § 162):

> In case (162) the meaning of the word 'derive' stood out clearly. But we told ourselves that this was only a quite special case of deriving; deriving in quite special clothing, which had to be stripped from it if we wanted to see the essence of deriving. So we stripped those particular coverings off; but then deriving itself disappeared. In order to find the real artichoke, we divested it of its leaves. For (162) was, to be sure, a special case of deriving; what is essential to deriving, however, was not hidden here beneath the exterior, but this "exterior" was one case out of the family of cases of deriving.
>
> And in the same way, we also use the word 'read' for a family of cases. And in different circumstances, we apply different criteria for a person's reading.[49]

Cook comments:

> One point to gather from this passage is that in so far as Wittgenstein uses the concept of criteria to oppose the notion of 'the hidden', this is *not* the notion that arises in the problem of other minds ... but rather that notion of the hidden that arises out of looking for a common element and finding none.[50]

In the end, I am unsure whether Cook thinks there *is* an important use for the term 'criterion' in philosophy.

## 4.4 Stanley Cavell

Criteria hold an important position in Stanley Cavell's reading of Wittgenstein.

Cavell has a sustained treatment of Wittgenstein's conception of criteria in his book *The Claim of Reason*.[51] He starts out by comparing non-philosophical, ordinary, uses and Wittgenstein's use of the word 'criterion'.

The idea of bringing up uses of the word 'criterion' in non-philosophical contexts is helpful in making the discussion more concrete. Among Cavell's examples are the following (I abbreviate his account for the present purpose) (8–9).

> A. 'American officials listed four criteria for judging a government here [in Saigon] as stable: ability to maintain law and order in the cities, the capacity to raise and support effective armed forces, an adequate degree of protection

---

[49] Also, consider the previous discussion about understanding.
[50] Canfield, *Wittgenstein*, 136.    [51] *The Claim of Reason* (1979).

for vital American and Vietnamese installations, and the presence of responsible officials . . . '

B. 'The sole criterion for me is whether it [a poem] can sweep me with it into
emotion . . . '

D. 'It is thus impracticable to use for the evaluation of an infantile neurosis
the same criteria which we apply in the care of an adult' (Anna Freud).

G. 'Among the main criteria for distinguishing the [social] strata from each
other [before the Great Depression and the Second World War] was their
respectability, their diligence and dutifulness, their capacity and readiness to
persist faithfully in a given task and their willingness to submit their performances to the assessment of authorities they regarded as legitimate.'

According to Cavell, Wittgensteinian criteria differ from ordinary criteria in
some important ways. In the case of ordinary criteria as opposed to
Wittgensteinian criteria, Cavell claims, there will be a distinction between criteria
and standards, criteria determining 'whether an object is (generally) of the right
kind, whether it is a relevant candidate at all, whereas standards discriminate the
degree to which a candidate satisfies those criteria' (11). (I am unsure to what
extent this distinction actually captures the contrast between ordinary and
Wittgensteinian criteria.) A second disanalogy is this:

In official cases in which criteria are appealed to, the object in question is one
that in some obvious way requires evaluation or assessment, one whose status
or ranking needs determining or settling. The point of setting up or establishing criteria is to allow these evaluations and decisions to be as rational
(consistent and coherent and impersonal and non-arbitrary) as possible.
Wittgenstein's candidates for judgment are not of this kind; they neither
raise nor permit an obvious question of evaluation or competitive status (14).

He then lists some of the things that, according to Wittgenstein, we appeal to
criteria to determine:

whether someone has a toothache, is sitting on a chair, is of an opinion, is
expecting someone between 4 and 4:30, was able to go on but no longer is; is
reading, thinking, believing, hoping, informing, following a rule; whether it's
raining; whether someone is talking to himself, attending to a shape or a color,
whether he means to be doing something, whether what he does is for him
done as a matter of course, etc.[52]

The contrast here does not seem altogether clear. Evidently, what Cavell calls
official criteria does not include the whole range of 'ordinary criteria'. For

---

[52] Ibid. We should note that not all of these examples are to be found in *Philosophical
Investigations*.

instance, case B would not seem to be expressive of a need to set up 'impersonal' criteria. On the other hand, among the Wittgensteinian criteria listed by Cavell, the question whether someone is reading, say, in the example Wittgenstein is considering, *is* a matter of evaluation.

The third disanalogy, according to Cavell, is this: where ordinary criteria are concerned, the authority for the criteria varies: in case A it is American officials, in case B it is the speaker, in case D it is the child-psychoanalyst Anna Freud, in case G, presumably, sociologists or historians (though the case is unclear).[53] By 'authority' I take it Cavell means whoever formulates or issues criteria – whether in a capacity of expert or decision maker. In the case of Wittgensteinian criteria, on the other hand, the authority is 'we':

> Wittgenstein's source of authority never varies in this way. It is, for him, always *we* who 'establish' the criteria under investigation. The criteria Wittgenstein appeals to – those which are, for him, the data of philosophy – are always 'ours', the 'group' which forms his 'authority' is always, apparently, the human group as such, the human being generally. When I voice them, I do so, or take myself to do so, as a member of that group, a representative human.[54]

Cavell then goes on to discuss the nature of the authority each of us has to speak for 'us'. Later on, he writes, 'In the case of Wittgensteinian criteria, we want to know the basis on which we grant any concept to anything, why we call things as we do' (29).[55] And then, speaking about what Wittgenstein calls grammatical investigations, he writes: 'what we discover in the course of such investigations, when we ask "Under what circumstances, or in what particular cases, do we say ... ?", are our criteria' (30).

Cavell accepts, as a central instance of criteria, criteria of pain, although unlike Malcolm he does not consider them to provide certain *knowledge* that another is in pain. It is from the criteria that we can tell that pain is *what is in question*, even if a person is just pretending to be in pain, play-acting, and so on. 'Criteria are "criteria for something's being so", not in the sense that they tell us of a thing's existence, but of something like its identity, not of its *being* so, but of its being *so*' (45).

Unlike ordinary criteria, Wittgensteinian criteria are, for Cavell, tied to concepts (words), thus, they have a generic character. He regards criteria as manifested in the life of humanity rather than specific languages. Cavell evidently construes it as a task of philosophical inquiry to discover criteria, and thus, in a sense, to establish deep truths about our language, about human language. On this point, he appears to deviate from the so-called therapeutic

---

[53] Cavell, *The Claim*, 18.      [54] Ibid.

[55] In this connection, Cavell also writes: 'our uses of language are pervasively, almost unimaginably, *systematic*.' The meaning of this claim is not clear to me.

view, with which he has often been associated. The therapeutic view emphasises the *ad hoc* nature of philosophical inquiry: rather than search for general observations about the nature of meaning, thought, understanding, sensation, and so on, the 'therapy-minded' philosopher addresses the particular bewilderments each of us may feel in the attempt to get clear about this or that specific issue. This is connected with the idea that to be free of our bewilderment, we have to try to think through the issue for ourselves: it is no use being provided with general principles, such as being told that the criteria for the application of this or that concept is such and such. Accordingly, if I am not badly mistaken, there is a tension here between Cavell's overall approach to philosophy and his discussion of the concept of criteria.

## 4.5 Gordon Baker and Peter Hacker

Peter Hacker is the commentator who, to my knowledge, has commented the most extensively and in the greatest detail on Wittgenstein's work on criteria. In the first (1972) edition of his book *Insight and Illusion*,[56] he argued that Wittgenstein's conception of criteria provided the ground for a new theory of meaning, based on assertion-conditions rather than truth-conditions (on this conception, the criteria for some phenomenon being satisfied does not entail that the phenomenon obtains, simply that you have a right to assert that it does, that is, in the circumstances, an error can be excused).[57] Similarly, in 1974, Gordon Baker (who would later work together with Hacker in writing a series of books commenting on the *Philosophical Investigations*), published a lively article[58] in which he argued that Wittgenstein's conception of criteria constituted a radically new type of semantics, 'Constructive Semantics', to replace the 'Classical Semantics' which had, according to Baker, in one form or another, been the predominant conception of meaning within analytic philosophy. As against what is held to be conceivable on the classical view, Baker argues, the criterial relation 'transmit[s] certainty from premise to conclusion', but this constitutes neither a deductive nor an inductive inference. Certainty is not to be identified with the impossibility of doubt. Considerations of knowledge and meaning are not separate but intertwined. As Baker concludes his article:

> It is a total misconception to ascribe to Wittgenstein the view that Classical Semantics is an incomplete account of meaning which must be filled out by adding a consideration of criteria. Along that course lies only the wreck of orthodox logical positivism. If the prevalence of this jargon were matched by

---

[56] Oxford: Clarendon Press, 1972. Reprinted in 1986.
[57] See 1986 edition, 322–35. For a critique of Hacker's 1972 conception, see Hunter, 'Critical Notice of P. M. S. Hacker's *Insight and Illusion*', 201–11.
[58] 'Criteria.'

an understanding of the theory on which it is based, then it would be true that Wittgenstein's concept of a criterion marked a turning point in the evolution of philosophy. We have witnessed not just the origin of a single species of semantics, but the emergence, as it were, of a whole new phylum. We have yet to recognize what it is that we have seen. (189)

In Baker and Hacker's joint work on Wittgenstein and in Hacker's later work, however, they abandoned the idea that Wittgenstein had been attempting to formulate a theory of meaning.[59] In 1993, Hacker wrote:

> It has been argued that [the concept of criteria] is a pivotal notion in Wittgenstein's later theory of meaning or semantics. Elaborating further, it has been suggested that it is embedded in an assertion-conditions or assertability-conditions theory of meaning which stands in contrast to Wittgenstein's earlier truth-conditional semantics . . .
> If the discussions and arguments of this Analytical Commentary approximate to Wittgenstein's intentions even remotely, it is clear that such interpretations are wildly off course.[60]

One rarely sees a philosopher distancing himself from his own earlier position more categorically.[61] He goes on:

> If we are to obtain a clear picture of [Wittgenstein's] use of the term 'criterion', we must eschew theory and engage in patient description.. . . . As we shall see [the term] converges substantially, though not uniformly, with the ordinary use of the word. It is not part of a *theory* of meaning, but a modest instrument in the description of the ways in which words are used. (546)

In my view, Hacker here takes up a fruitful attitude to Wittgenstein's use of 'criterion'. He lists what he calls the rough outlines of Wittgenstein's view: criteria are involved in the grammar of the expressions for which they are criteria; they are aspects of the meaning of those expressions; they are grounds for asserting propositions; in some cases, there are multiple criteria; in some cases, criteria are defeasible (555). In all, Hacker observes,

> it is not possible to give a uniform account of [Wittgenstein's] notion of a criterion. In some contexts a criterion amounts to a sufficient condition, whereas in others it constitutes grammatically determined presumptive grounds.... But it is only if one is misguided enough to think that this conception of a grammatical criterion is part of a novel theory of

---

[59] Baker & Hacker, *Wittgenstein: Understanding and Meaning*; *Wittgenstein: Rules, Grammar and Necessity*.

[60] Hacker, *Wittgenstein: Meaning and Mind*, 545. See also the Preface to Hacker, *Insight and Illusion*, Revised ed., vii–viii.

[61] Another instance may be Rogers Albritton, in the 1966 postscript to his "On Wittgenstein's Use", 247–59, although I find his presentation less than transparent.

meaning ... that one need find any incoherence here.... [The] grammatical features of criteria vary from one language-game to another. It should not be expected that what counts as a criterion for the truth of a mathematical proposition should share all the logico-grammatical features for the truth of psychological propositions. (561)[62]

# 5 Some Issues in the Debate about Criteria

It may be helpful, at this point, to note some of the ways in which the role of criterial claims and criterial conditions, whether in everyday life or in philosophy, may vary. In much of the post-Wittgensteinian debate about criteria, these variations tend to be disregarded. Discussion is often carried on at an abstract level with little attention paid to the particulars of the various cases in which questions about criteria may be raised. (In some cases, criterial relations are simply referred to with symbolic variables.[63]) In following this practice, one runs the danger of letting one's thinking be governed, more or less unconsciously, by the cases that happen to be at the back of one's mind. I want to bring into the open some of the issues and unspoken assumptions which have underlain the post-Wittgensteinian debate about criteria and which may account for some of the main lines of disagreement. I will leave aside talk of criteria in mathematics, and focus primarily on the nature of criterial claims in connection with things said about human beings, their actions, abilities, experiences, motives, and so on.[64]

## 5.1 Paradigmatic Uses

A question which is sometimes touched upon in passing but is not delved into by participants in the debate is that of the relation between the role of criteria in everyday (and scientific) language and Wittgenstein's use of the notion. (The exception here is Stanley Cavell, who argues that Wittgensteinian criteria are clearly distinct from criteria as spoken of outside philosophy. However, Cavell's conception of Wittgenstein's use of the word appears to be rather too unified.) Some of the uses of criteria discussed by Wittgenstein concern cases in which a person is instructed in some skill or ability, such as being taught to read, to recite the alphabet, or to play chess. In these cases, Wittgenstein's use of the word 'criterion' seems to correspond closely to common ways of speaking outside philosophy. In saying this, it should be noted, I am not suggesting that

---

[62] For a thoughtful discussion along similar lines, see Bennett, "Wittgenstein and Defining Criteria", 49–63.

[63] Compare, e.g. Chihara & Fodor, 'Operationalism and Ordinary Language', 281–95; Lycan, 'Non-Inductive Evidence', 109–51; Baker, 'Criteria'; Canfield, *Wittgenstein*.

[64] Criteria in mathematics do not appear to give rise to problems of interpretation.

the *word* 'criterion' will necessarily be used in those everyday situations: the point is rather that we can easily identify ways of speaking and proceeding in which certain performances hold a 'criterial role'. What characterizes these situations, we might say, is the *importance of settling* the issue whether the pupil has acquired the skill in question, say, when it comes to deciding whether the instruction should be continued, or whether she can be assigned certain tasks or be admitted to certain activities. Here we often look for a yes-or-no resolution. For certain purposes, we may even stipulate an exact standard. In *PI* I, § 157, Wittgenstein writes: 'Which was the first word that he *read*? This question makes no sense here. Unless, indeed, we stipulate: "The first word that a person 'reads' is the first word of the first series of 50 words that he reads correctly" (or something of the sort).'

The cases in which definite resolutions are called for are often, but not always, cases in which it is a question of coming up to a standard, in the sense of a person attempting to qualify for a category. Among other practices which are similarly characterized by a need for resolutions are legal matters ('Who is the rightful owner of this property?', 'Was he really culpable?') or games ('Was this a goal?', 'Was that a strike?').

I would like to suggest that this type of context is, in some sense, paradigmatic of criterial claims or criterial thought patterns in ordinary human intercourse. This is also the type of context where ordinary criterial considerations and Wittgenstein's use of criteria correspond the most closely to one another.[65]

On the other hand, let is consider a context in which there normally is no call for a definite resolution. Suppose I assert that John is homesick or that Martha is xenophobic. You may wish to question my judgment, yet in such a case you would not normally raise the question of what criteria I apply, or what ways of acting or expressing oneself is to be given a criterial role, even when the grounds given by the other in support of his view leads you to believe that he and you were talking at cross purposes. The discussion, in this case, has a different *form* than in the cases mentioned before: even if we are unable to agree, the discussion may be illuminating, say, in our coming to have a better understanding of the person we are talking about, through the observations and reflections we may advance in support of our diverging opinions.

An interesting case in this connection is Wittgenstein's discussion about the criteria of love in a much earlier connection: in a lecture in 1934 recorded by Alice Ambrose and Margaret MacDonald.[66] He talks about the mental cramp that may be produced by the failure to distinguish between two statements that

---

[65] Compare here Hanfling's notion of the 'constitutive sense' of criteria, in his 'Criteria', 42–3.
[66] *Wittgenstein's Lectures 1932–1935.* The relevant passage is on pp. 90–1.

are closely connected, where one is an 'experiential proposition' and the other is a 'rule':

> Suppose it is said that A loves B, meaning that he has certain feelings for B, but that when B's life is endangered and A could have saved him, he did not. We say, 'This cannot have been love.' Has the statement 'A loves B' been contradicted by A's not saving his life? No. It is not a contradiction to say that A had the feeling for B but did not save him. It is only a conjecture that whenever A has a certain feeling he will do so-and-so in the future. But it is quite another thing to say I am not going to *call* this love if A did not save B when he could have done so. 'If A had loved B he would have saved him' is not an experiential statement at all, but a definition or explication of what I call love. If as a matter of fact a certain feeling almost always goes together with a certain behavior, we are inclined to use feeling and behavior alternatively as criteria for love.... Behavior and feeling are very often found together, so that we are inclined to give both phenomena the name 'love' athough they are different criteria.

The case of love is interesting because of the way some uses of the word 'love' differs from the use of words like 'homesickness' and 'xenophobia'. There is an important way of talking about love in which, apart from questions of feeling and behaviour, the question of love is a question of commitment to a relationship (say, between partners). The question whether the other's love for me is genuine may be one that calls for an urgent decision. Later on, Wittgenstein wrote: 'Love is not a feeling. Love is put to the test, pain is not'[67], and

> 'If it passes, then it was not true love.' Why *was* it not in that case? Is it our experience, that only this feeling and not that endures? Or are we using a picture: we test love for its *inner* character, which the immediate feeling does not discover. Still, this picture is important to us. Love, what is important, is not a feeling, but something deeper, which only manifests itself in the feeling.[68]

While Wittgenstein here seems to rely on a rather restricted use of the word 'feeling' which might be questioned, he is noting that talk of love, especially as it may arise *between* partners – in contrast to talk about most other emotions – in many cases shares some features with talk about abilities, about coming up to a standard. This, it appears, could make room for talk about criteria of love, even though those are criteria that could hardly be formulated in general terms, but would rather be specific to an individual.

Next, let us think about the word 'pain' which has become something of a standard case in post-Wittgensteinian discussions of criteria. (Wittgenstein himself discusses the criteria of toothache in *The Brown Book*; in *Philosophical*

---

[67] Wittgenstein, *Remarks on the Philosophy of Psychology*, § 959.   [68] Ibid., § 115.

*Investigations*, however, there is no discussion of the criteria of pain, only, in one case, of two people having the same pain.) In the discussion, things such as groaning, wincing, or writhing are often mentioned as criteria of pain. However, in everyday talk about pain there is no unified notion of what behaviours hold a criterial role. For instance, if asked whether this or that was a criterion or a symptom of pain, we might be at a loss for an answer. When it comes to pain behaviour, we might say, there does not appear to be a centre of variation from which specific instances may deviate to a greater or lesser extent. Rather, there is a myriad of physiognomies of pain, expressions of pain varying depending on the character of the pain, its intensity, location, and the circumstances in which it occurs or the situation in which the pain is expressed.[69]

The contexts in which pain language is normally taught and primarily used are contexts of concern: we often respond to expressions of pain by showing pity, by trying to alleviate the sufferer's condition or by sparing her from exertions that might tend to worsen her pain. We could say: here it is not a question of coming up to a standard. It is only where there is room for suspecting that someone might be simulating pain (say, a malingering soldier) that we would talk, say, about someone's expression of pain being convincing or unconvincing. The nature of the decision called for when there is a question of someone being in pain is wholly different from the decision needed when it is a question, say, of being able to read.

In the case of pain, we would not be likely to ask the sort of question I mentioned in the Introduction: 'When do we say ... ?', 'How does one tell ... ?' or 'What is it one calls ... ?' Genuine pain is not a context in which talk of *specific* criterial considerations sits naturally, nor does it appear to be central to Wittgenstein's conception of criteria in *Philosophical Investigations*.[70]

## 5.2 General vs Particular Criterial Claims

It may be useful to distinguish between general criterial claims that have the role of clarifying the common use of some term within a practice (whether or not explicitly making use of the word 'criterion') and claims to the effect that in a particular situation such and such was a criterion of something being so. In the cases that I suggested might be considered paradigmatic for criteria talk – skills, games, legal contexts – criterial claims of the first kind are common. They are usually made with the unspoken understanding that the application of the criteria is dependent on the circumstances being normal. For the most part, of

---

[69] For an illuminating discussion of human and animal expression, see Cockburn, '"Only of a Living Human Being"', 57–70.
[70] There is an argument along similar lines in Hanfling, 'Criteria', 41–5.

course, it will be thought neither possible nor necessary to give a complete account of which circumstances will not be considered normal. We might say, these claims are made against the background of a shared understanding of the practice in question, and thus, of the kinds of circumstances that might count against the application of the term even when events conform to the condition.

In discussing Gordon Baker's essay 'Criteria: A New Foundation for Semantics', John McDowell writes:

> Baker's assumption is evidently this: if a condition is ever a criterion for a claim, by virtue of belonging to some type of condition that can be ascertained to obtain independently of establishing the claim, then any condition of that type constitutes a criterion for that claim, or one suitably related to it. Given that such a condition obtains, further circumstances determine whether the support it affords the claim is solid; if the further circumstances are unfavourable, we still have, according to this view, a case of a criterion's being satisfied, but the support it affords the claim is defeated. But when Wittgenstein speaks of dependence on circumstances, what he says seems to permit a different reading: not that some condition, specified in terms that are applicable independently of establishing a claim, is a criterion for the claim anyway . . ., but that whether such a condition is a criterion or not depends on the circumstances.[71]

McDowell provides a striking illustration of his point:

> In a schematic picture of a face, it may be the curve of the mouth that makes it right to say that the face is cheerful. In another picture the mouth may be represented by a perfect replica of the line that represents the mouth in the first picture, although the face is not cheerful. Do we need a relation of defeasible support in order to accommodate this possibility? Surely not. What is in question is the relation of 'making it right to say'; it holds in the first case and not in the second. Since the relation does not hold in the second case, it cannot be understood in terms of entailment. But why suppose the only alternative is defeasible support? That would require assuming that the warranting status we are concerned with must be shared by all members of a type to which the warranting circumstance can be ascertained to belong independently of the claim it warrants. . . . That assumption looks in this case like baseless prejudice; perhaps the generalized version of it, which yields the conception of criteria that I am questioning, is similarly baseless.[72]

This reading runs against the noninductive evidence view formulated by Shoemaker. Something *counts* as a criterion only in certain circumstances.

---

[71] McDowell, 'Criteria'. The quotation is from p. 377.
[72] Ibid., p. 378. McDowell says that the example is inspired by Malcolm's essay 'Wittgenstein on the Nature of Mind', 133–58. The example occurs on p. 139. (Malcom's essay is one of the most illuminating overviews of Wittgenstein's thinking about the philosophy of mind that I know of.)

There are no criteria here that may be 'defeated' by the circumstances. (I would suggest, however, that it would, on that conception, be misleading to say, as Canfield does, that a criterion being met is 'decisive' for something being the case. To say that the criterion was met is already to have decided the matter.)

However, it may be asked whether McDowell is not here talking at cross-purposes with Shoemaker and Baker. It appears that what they have in mind are different types of criterial claims, as outlined here. What Shoemaker and Baker are talking about, it appears, are the kinds of criterial claims that could be made in advance, or could be formulated on a general level, whereas McDowell is focusing on cases in which we call something a criterion in a particular instance *because* we are satisfied that the condition for which it is a criterion obtains. Criterial claims of the former, general kind could well be considered defeasible.

In the case of stereotypical 'emoji' faces (of the kind envisaged by Malcolm and McDowell), it would not in fact be hard to formulate advance – hence defeasible – criteria for how they are to be read. When it comes to the artistic rendering of an expression in a painting, on the other hand, the idea of any such advance criteria would seem out of place (if a painter used some standard trick to convey an expression that would certainly be held against him) – in that case, on the other hand, we might doubt whether there would be any room for talk of *criteria* for interpreting the sitter's expression; we either see it or we do not.

Actually, analogous considerations apply to Cook's example of expecting someone: his point is that the expecting may manifest itself in an indefinite variety of ways depending on the situation (cp. Section 4.3). Talk about expectation, in this respect, is rather different from attributions of ability. Possibly Cook means to suggest that in this case there is no use for questions about criteria. Maybe we could say: in criterial talk there is always a hint towards some generality – whether that generality is one that could fruitfully be captured in a verbal formulation varies from case to case. The idea of defeasibility is connected with general claims.

## 5.3 Indeterminate and Shifting Criteria

After the passage from *The Blue Book* quoted in the previous section, Wittgenstein goes on to complicate the picture:

> In practice, if you were asked which phenomenon is the defining criterion and which is a symptom, you would in most cases be unable to answer this question except by making an arbitrary decision *ad hoc*. It may be practical to define a word by taking one phenomenon as the defining criterion, but we shall easily be persuaded to define the word by means of what, according to

our first use, was a symptom. Doctors will use names of diseases without ever deciding which phenomena are to be taken as criteria and which as symptoms; and this need not be a deplorable lack of clarity. For remember that in general we don't use language according to strict rules – it hasn't been taught us by means of strict rules either.[73]

Wittgenstein, then, suggests that the criteria/symptom distinction may be indeterminate or that it may shift, that criterial claims may be formulated as an afterthought, and that they may be based on a decision. It is not obvious, in the context, whether he means for this observation to apply only to concepts like angina, or whether it is supposed to extend to all contexts in which criteria are talked about. Similar themes are broached in *Philosophical Investigations.* Thus, *PI* I, § 79 concludes with the following words in parentheses: 'The fluctuation of scientific definitions: what today counts as an observed concomitant of phenomenon A will to-morrow be used to define "A."'

This remark is preceded by a discussion of the use of the name Moses in referring to the character in the *Old Testament.* Wittgenstein's point (as I would render it) is that we may unproblematically refer to Moses even though it is indeterminate exactly what things currently taken to be true of him would have to hold for conversation about him to continue without disruption. The analogy, evidently, is that in natural science there may be a shift between defining marks and empirical evidence of some phenomenon without this creating a disruption in the discourse.[74]

---

[73] Wittgenstein, *The Blue Book*, 25.

[74] *PI* I, § 354 begins as follows: 'The fluctuation in grammar between criteria and symptoms makes it look as if there were nothing at all but symptoms.'
However, the ensuing remark is not really an illustration of this idea:

> We say, for example: 'Experience teaches that there is rain when the barometer falls, but it also teaches that there is rain when we have certain feelings of wet and cold, or such-and-such visual impressions.' As an argument in support of this, one says that these sense-impressions can deceive us. But here one overlooks the fact that their deceiving us precisely about rain rests on a definition.

For a comment on this somewhat confusing remark, see Hacker, *Wittgenstein: Meaning and Mind*, p 383. Hacker points out that this remark is preceded by the following remark in MS-115, 72[3]:

> How does one know whether it is raining? We see, feel, the rain. The meaning of the word 'rain' is explained to us with those experiences. I say, they are 'criteria' for its raining. 'What is rain?' and 'What does rain look like?' are logically related questions. If experience has taught us that a sudden fall of the barometer always goes together with rainfall, then I shall consider such a barometer fall as a *symptom* of rainfall. Whether a phenomenon is a symptom of rain is taught by experience, what counts as a criterion of rain is a matter of stipulation (definition)/ our determination. (Translation by Hacker.)

In fact, Wittgenstein broaches two different though related themes in these remarks. First, there is a point about indeterminacy: at any given point in time, an individual participant in a practice might not be prepared to distinguish between what is criterial and what is simply symptomatic of a phenomenon being spoken about. For instance, if he were asked 'If this experiment had such and such an unexpected outcome, would you still call this an X?' he might simply shrug his shoulders, or he might say, 'It *won't happen*'. This might also be true of the members of the community in general. If a set of characteristics tend to go together, there may never be a practical need for deciding which circumstance is to be regarded as criterial. This is true, for instance, when it comes to certain diseases. Something similar will hold, on the whole, when it comes to various phenomena studied in the natural sciences.

The second point concerns variability: what were considered criteria of a phenomenon at some point in time may later unproblematically come to be regarded as symptoms, and vice versa. One can imagine that, often enough, during the transition, there was a period when the criteria/symptoms distinction was indeterminate. An example of this type of transition, I think, would be the concept of a gene in biology. In 1909, the Danish botanist Wilhelm Johannsen coined the word 'gene' to describe the factors, discovered by Gregor Mendel, in accordance with which traits were inherited from parents to offspring among plants and animals. The physiological constitution of these factors, however, was left to be investigated empirically. In 2022, on the other hand, the word 'gene' is defined as follows in the *Merriam-Webster* online dictionary:

> a specific sequence of nucleotides in DNA or RNA that is located usually on a chromosome and that is the functional unit of inheritance controlling the transmission and expression of one or more traits by specifying the structure of a particular polypeptide and especially a protein or controlling the function of other genetic material.[75]

Here we can see how the results of empirical research – not least Francis Crick and James D. Watson's discovery of the structure of the DNA molecule – have come to be incorporated into the very concept of the gene – at the same time, the line between what is criterial and what is incidental is apparently fluid at present. Even so, there does not seem to have been any crack in the progress of genetic research. Here we have a case of variation combined with indeterminacy.

---

This remark, it seems, succeeds in bringing out what Wittgenstein is trying to say more clearly than § 354.

[75] www.merriam-webster.com/dictionary/gene. Accessed 16 February 2022.

Can this be extended to a general point about the nature of criteria? In Section 1.1, I discussed the suggestion that the criteria for a skill such as knowing the alphabet might be changed from performance to brain state. The point was made that such a shift would carry with it a radical change in the role of talking about this skill in human intercourse – or maybe we should say: one way of talking would be abolished, and another one, which happened to be homonymous with the first, would be introduced. Analogously, there seems to be limited leeway for the degree to which criteria of knowing the alphabet might be indeterminate. In a given context, one might fix on a specific standard for attributing the skill to someone, but even then, the proposed standard would be constrained by the general framework within which this skill is commonly assessed – otherwise, it is hard to see what the standard would have to do with what is commonly meant by knowing the alphabet. Unlike what is the case with the word 'gene' within genetics, a switch to a neurological criterion for knowledge of the alphabet would indeed cause a rupture in our ways of dealing with one another. Similar considerations would seem to apply to much of our talk about human abilities. Analogous points can be made as well about words connected with questions of entitlement, legal obligations, and the like: say, coming of age, ownership, debt. Living in a house is often connected with ownership, but there is rarely any unclarity on whether the person who has acquired a house or the person who lives in it is to be considered the owner.

In as far as research within the natural sciences is concerned with correlations between phenomena, with detecting dependencies, and with making predictions, the distinction between criteria and empirical evidence may often not be crucial. It might be suggested that this is so to the extent to which the world of natural science, unlike the human life-world, is, in a sense, 'flat' from a human point of view. When physical and chemical phenomena touch human practical (or symbolic) concerns, however, the distinction becomes crucial, as when we ask whether a fabric is flammable, whether a substance is poisonous, whether a material is biodegradable – or where, when it comes to the beginning or end of the life of a human being, we are to draw the line between life and death.

What about a word like 'pain'? I argued before that criterial claims do not, for the most part, sit naturally with discussions of whether someone is in pain. Even so, I would claim that a distinction *like* that between criteria and symptoms undeniably has a place in connection with ascriptions of pain, and that the idea of a shift between what is 'criterial' and what is symptomatic when it comes to ascriptions of pain is unrealistic.

Even if, as I have argued, there would be no point in trying to list the expressions that are criterial of pain, I would claim that only statements in which the grammatical subject is a human being or an animal – as opposed to some organ or body part – will come up for consideration as criterial. In some contexts, certain reactions of the sympathetic nervous system, such as the psychogalvanic reflex, are regarded as symptomatic of pain. Obviously, these symptoms have been established by appeals to test subjects' expressions of pain. Again, there is a debate among neuroscientists concerning which parts of the brain are involved in feeling pain, and in this case, too, individuals' expressions of pain will have to be invoked in trying to settle the debate.[76]

Now, suppose we tried to imagine a language (otherwise like English) in which reactions of the sympathetic nervous system or occurrences in the brain were regarded as criteria of 'pain'. Coming to do so would involve a huge shift (if 'shift' is indeed the right word) in the way the word 'pain' is used. A person's verbal expressions of pain and her pain behaviour would then be treated as symptomatic of pain, but the question of whether she really did have – we could hardly say 'feel' – pain would be left up to a neurological investigation. In this case, the place of 'pain' talk in human life would, of course, be totally different from what it is today. Maybe we could try to imagine this happening in consequence of a scientistic fad. However, it is not really clear what such a science fiction scenario would actually come to. It is likely, I suppose, that some new form of expression would be introduced taking the place currently held by pain talk in human society (rather than saying 'My leg hurts', people might say 'It's as if I had a pain in my leg', and then others would pity them just as they do now; in that case, the conceptual shift would be illusory).

David Cockburn suggested to me in discussion that we might consider the possibility of neurological criteria of pain being used side by side with human expression. This possibility is indeed worth considering. Now, it would make a huge difference whether one is thinking of a case in which the neurological criteria could *overrule* expressions of pain – in which case the scenario would be as described in the previous paragraph – or whether they would be invoked in cases in which expressions were mute. The latter might be the case, say, where people are unconscious or totally paralyzed and thus unable to express pain, or in the case of animals – maybe even plants – that do not have expressive behaviour (or whose expressive behaviour we are unable to discern). The question then is whether we could take seriously the notion that in those cases neurological or other physiological conditions could become criterial for attributions of pain. At bottom, that is a question of whether in these cases we would respond to the person or the organism the way we do to someone expressing behaviour in familiar ways. My inclination would be to say that here we have a case of indeterminacy: in these cases we can equally imagine different ways of responding.

---

[76] Kwon, 'The Battle over Pain in the Brain'.

## Conclusion

In the Introduction, I raised the question of why interest in Wittgenstein's use of the term 'criterion' has waned over time since the publication of *Philosophical Investigations*. I believe I may now provide some hints for an answer. On being posthumously published, this work created a great stir within analytic philosophy and was seen as a challenge to some of its deepest-held assumptions. And indeed, this perception was in many ways well-grounded. The task of philosophy had been taken to be the laying bare of the logical structures of sentences as determined by the words of which the sentences are composed. In contrast to this, Wittgenstein in *Philosophical Investigations* emphasized the actual use of words in particular contexts. The sense of words and utterances was constituted by their place in the practices in which they were used.

It was commonly thought that Wittgenstein's use of the term 'criterion' provided the key to what was revolutionary in his approach to philosophy. It offered a conception of logical relations between utterances that was more flexible, more context-dependent than that commonly taken for granted within the analytical tradition. However, the debate has revealed that the centrality of criteria for clarifying Wittgenstein's thinking was overrated. For one thing, there was unclarity about what criteria actually were. How was Wittgenstein's use of the term related to its non-philosophical use? In speaking about the criteria for this or that assertion, was Wittgenstein assuming that that was the terminology that users of the language would use, and if not, what was the mode of existence of criteria? Second, criterial claims seemed not to constitute a unified notion. The role of 'criteria' differed depending on whether what was discussed were mathematical expressions, concepts in natural science, or the psychological concepts of everyday life (and there were differences within the latter category as well). Also, it was unclear whether criterial claims were to be taken to be general, or whether they only applied in particular instances. Third, where criteria were invoked in the discussion of various philosophical problems, such as other minds or private language, the interesting issues did not concern the concept of criteria as such but whatever use of words appeals to criteria were meant to illuminate. Hence the term 'criterion' seemed not to be indispensable for discussing the problems in question. In some cases, writers have replaced the distinction between criterial and evidentiary relations with the distinction between internal and external relations between assertions.

All the same, the post-Wittgensteinian debate about criteria has been useful. It has provided an opportunity for venting the presuppositions underlying discussions about language, meaning, and the philosophy of mind. It has also provided an incitement to subjecting Wittgenstein's later work to close scrutiny and to bringing out the contrasts between Wittgenstein's thought and analytical philosophy in its more traditional forms. The term 'criterion' does not provide the only way of helping us focus on actual uses of language in all their variety, but it certainly does provide one way of doing so.

# Bibliography

Albritton, Rogers (1968). 'On Wittgenstein's Use of the Term "Criterion"'. In George Pitcher (ed.), *Wittgenstein: The Philosophical Investigations*. London: University of Notre Dame Press, 231–50.

Ambrose, Alice, ed. (1979). *Wittgenstein's Lectures, Cambridge 1932–1935: From the notes of Alice Ambrose and Margaret MacDonald*. Chicago: University of Chicago Press.

Baker, G. P. (1974). 'Criteria: A New Foundation for Semantics'. *Ratio* 16 (1974), 156–89. Reprinted in Canfield 1986.

Baker, G. P. (2004). *Wittgenstein's Method: Neglected Aspects*. Oxford: Basil Blackwell.

Baker, G. P. & P. M. S. Hacker (1985). *Wittgenstein: Rules, Grammar and Necessity*. Oxford: Basil Blackwell.

Baker, G. P. & P. M. S. Hacker (1980). *Wittgenstein: Understanding and Meaning*. Oxford: Basil Blackwell.

Bennett, Philip W. (1978). 'Wittgenstein and Defining Criteria'. *Philosophical Investigations* 1, 9–63. Reprinted in Canfield 1986.

Canfield, John V., ed. (1986). *The Philosophy of Wittgenstein. Vol. 7: Criteria*. New York: Garland Publishing.

Canfield, John V. (1981). *Wittgenstein: Language and World*. Amherst: University of Massachusetts Press.

Cavell, Stanley (1979). *The Claim of Reason: Wittgenstein, Skepticism, Morality, and Tragedy*. Oxford: Oxford University Press.

Chihara, Charles S. & Jerry A. Fodor (1965). 'Operationalism and Ordinary Language: A Critique of Wittgenstein'. *American Philosophical Quarterly* 2, 281–95. Reprinted in Canfield 1986.

Cockburn, David (2021). '"Only of a Living Human Being"'. In *Wittgenstein, Human Beings and Conversation*. London: Anthem Press, 57–69.

Cook, John (1969). 'Human Beings'. In Peter Winch (ed.), *Studies in the Philosophy of Wittgenstein*. London: Routledge & Kegan Paul, 117–51.

'gene' (2022). www.merriam-webster.com/dictionary/gene. Accessed 16 February 2022.

Glock, Hans-Johann (1996). *A Wittgenstein Dictionary*. Oxford: Basil Blackwell.

Hacker, P. M. S. (1972). *Insight and Illusion*. Oxford: Clarendon Press.

Hacker, P. M. S. (1997). *Insight and Illusion: Themes in the Philosophy of Wittgenstein*. Revised ed. Bristol: Thoemmes Press.

Hacker, P. M. S. (1990). *Wittgenstein: Meaning and Mind*. Oxford: Basil Blackwell.

Hacker, P. M. S. (1996). *Wittgenstein: Mind and Will*. Oxford: Basil Blackwell.

Hanfling, Oswald (2002). 'Criteria, Conventions and the Problem of Other Minds'. In *Wittgenstein and the Human Form of Life*. London: Routledge, 38–50.

Hertzberg, Lars (2022). 'The Need for a Listener and Community Standards'. In *Wittgenstein and the Life We Live with Language*. London: Anthem Press, 73–86.

Hunter, John F. M. (1974). 'Critical Notice of P. M. S. Hacker's *Insight and Illusion*'. *Canadian Journal of Philosophy* 4, 201–11. Reprinted in Canfield 1986.

Hunter, John F. M. (1977). 'Wittgenstein on Inner Processes and Outward Criteria'. *Canadian Journal of Philosophy* 7, 805–17. Reprinted in Canfield 1986.

Kenny, Anthony (1967). 'Criterion'. In Paul Edwards (ed.), *Encyclopedia of Philosophy*, vol. 2. New York: Macmillan, 258–61.

Kwon, Diana (2022). 'The Battle over Pain in the Brain'. www.scientificamerican .com/article/the-battle-over-pain-in-the-brain/. Accessed 28 January 2022.

Loomis, Eric (2010). 'Criteria'. In Kelly Dean Jolly (ed.), *Wittgenstein: Key Concepts*. Durham: Acumen, 160–8.

Lycan, W. Gregory (1971). 'Non-inductive Evidence: Recent Work on Wittgenstein's "Criteria"'. *American Philosophical Quarterly* 8, 109–51. Reprinted in Canfield 1986.

Malcolm, Norman (1963). *Knowledge and Certainty*. Englewood Cliffs, NJ: Prentice Hall.

Malcolm, Norman (1986). *Nothing Is Hidden: Wittgenstein's Criticism of His Early Thought*. Oxford: Basil Blackwell.

Malcolm, Norman (1977). 'Wittgenstein on the Nature of Mind.' In Malcolm, *Thought and Knowledge*. Ithaca: Cornell University Press, 133–58.

Malcolm, Norman. (1968). 'Wittgenstein's *Philosophical Investigations*'. In George Pitcher (ed.), *Wittgenstein:* The Philosophical Investigations. London: University of Notre Dame Press, 65–103.

McDowell, John (1998). 'Criteria, Defeasibility and Knowledge'. In *Meaning, Knowledge and Reality*. Cambridge, MA: Harvard University Press, 369–94.

Rhees, Rush (1998). 'Wittgenstein's Builders.' In D. Z. Phillips (ed.), *Wittgenstein and the Possibility of Discourse*. Cambridge: Cambridge University Press, 178–97.

Shoemaker, Sydney (1963). *Self-Knowledge and Self-Identity*. Ithaca, NY: Cornell University Press.

Wittgenstein, Ludwig (1958). *The Blue and Brown Books*. New York: Harper Row.

Wittgenstein, Ludwig (1968). *Philosophical Investigations*. 3rd ed., translated by G. E. M. Anscombe. Oxford: Basil Blackwell [1953].

Wittgenstein, Ludwig (2009a). *Philosophical Investigations*. 4th ed., translated by G. E. M. Anscombe, P. M. S. Hacker, and Joachim Schulte. Chichester: Wiley-Blackwell [1953].

Wittgenstein, Ludwig (2009b). *Philosophy of Psychology: A Fragment* (previously known as "Part II".) In Wittgenstein (2009a.)

Wittgenstein, Ludwig (1980). *Remarks on the Philosophy of Psychology*, vol. 1. Oxford: Basil Backwell.

Wittgenstein, Ludwig (1961). *Tractatus Logico-Philosophicus*, translated by D. F. Pears & B. F. McGuinness. London: Routledge and Kegan Paul [1921].

Wittgenstein, Ludwig (1967). *Zettel*. Oxford: Basil Blackwell.

Wright, Crispin (1993). *Realism, Meaning and Truth*, 2nd ed. Oxford: Basil Blackwell.

# Acknowledgement

I wish to thank David Cockburn who read most of the manuscript and offered invaluable advice both on matters of substance and of presentation. I also wish to thank series editor David Stern and two anonymous referees for helpful comments on the manuscript.

Cambridge Elements ⹀

# The Philosophy of Ludwig Wittgenstein

David G. Stern

*University of Iowa*

David G. Stern is Professor of Philosophy and Collegiate Fellow in the College of Liberal Arts
and Sciences at the University of Iowa. His research interests include history of analytic
philosophy, philosophy of language, philosophy of mind, and philosophy of science. He is
the author of *Wittgenstein's Philosophical Investigations: An Introduction* (Cambridge
University Press, 2004) and *Wittgenstein on Mind and Language* (Oxford University Press,
1995), as well as more than fifty journal articles and book chapters. He is the editor of
*Wittgenstein in the 1930s: Between the 'Tractatus' and the 'Investigations'* (Cambridge
University Press, 2018) and is also a co-editor of the *Cambridge Companion to Wittgenstein*
(Cambridge University Press, 2nd edition, 2018), *Wittgenstein: Lectures, Cambridge
1930–1933, from the Notes of G. E. Moore* (Cambridge University Press, 2016) and
*Wittgenstein Reads Weininger* (Cambridge University Press, 2004).

## About the Series

This series provides concise and structured introductions to all the central topics in the
philosophy of Ludwig Wittgenstein. The Elements are written by distinguished senior
scholars and bright junior scholars with relevant expertise, producing balanced and
comprehensive coverage of the full range of Wittgenstein's thought.

Cambridge Elements $\equiv$

# The Philosophy of Ludwig Wittgenstein

## Elements in the Series

Printed in the United States
by Baker & Taylor Publisher Services